UNYOKED

Overcoming Divorce

With Christian Courage

WORKBOOK

By

Todd Turner

Table of Contents

To the ultimate endurers, my mom & sister

FOREWORD
By Harmony Dust

I am no stranger to heartbreak and trauma. After surviving a childhood riddled with abuse and neglect, I became susceptible to an exploiter. The relationship was physically and emotionally abusive and led me down a very dark path of working in strip clubs under his control.

Enter Jesus.

The healing and transformation I experienced as a result of walking with Jesus cannot be overstated. I found a path to recovery and permanent freedom from exploitation. Discovering the truth that God can use our pain for purpose, I founded Treasures, an organization that empowers women who have experienced exploitation and trafficking in the commercial sex industry to live healthy and flourishing lives.

Mixed into all of the beautiful truths and revelations that brought about so much transformation in my life was one false belief - I thought that Christianity provided the perfect formula for the perfect life. I believed that as long as I followed all the rules and did everything right, my life would be filled with abundance and blessings at all times.

You can imagine my utter dismay when I discovered my first husband was having affairs and unwilling to do the hard work to repair our marriage. We read all the right books, went to premarital counseling, attended connect groups and did "all of the things." And yet, I still found myself heartbroken and abandoned.

I called my church to ask if there was someone, *anyone*, I could talk to that had gone through this and made it to the other end.

"I *do* know someone who has gone through this. But unfortunately, they aren't willing to talk about it." The pastor said regretfully.

A sense of utter loneliness and hopelessness struck me to the marrow of my bones.

Ultimately, I found support to get me through. Celebrate Recovery was profoundly helpful in addressing cycles of codependency that had wreaked havoc in my marriage. Grief Recovery helped me process my pain and find closure.

Eventually, filled with an abundance of hope, I married again.

And divorced again.

I did not want this story. This was not the outcome I expected when I vowed to love until my last breath. And yet, here I am.

The second divorce was no less painful, but I was less alone and just a little less hopeless. I have a beautiful community of friends that have wiped my tears and lifted my head. They have helped me return to myself, again. I also have more tools to process the pain and the grief.

Today, I have a faith that understands that sorrow and suffering are a part of life on this earth. And, although God does not always deliver us from the experience of suffering, He is always always *with us* in our suffering.

If you are walking through the aftermath of a divorce, you may feel like life as you know it is falling apart. You are not alone in your pain. There are no easy answers or quick-fix solutions, but my hope is that the pages of this workbook will encourage you that there *is* a way through. I know from experience that you can find your way back to the beauty and joy life has to offer.

Harmony Dust
Author of Scars and Stilettos
Founder & Executive Director of Treasures
www.iamatreasure.com
@iamharmonydust @Treasures.LA

Preface

As I pen down these words, I am acutely aware of the myriad of emotions and challenges that accompany the journey through divorce, for men and for women. This preface serves as an intimate invitation into the heart of the "Christian Divorce Recovery Workbook for Women." It's a space where our shared experiences converge, where the pages unfold as a source of solace, guidance, and empowerment.

A Personal Reflection:

My own divorce journey, fraught with pain and uncertainty, laid the foundation for this workbook. In those trying moments, I longed for resources that resonated with the intricacies of Christian faith, delving into the emotional and spiritual facets often overlooked. The absence of such tailored support sparked a desire within me to create a companion to my Unyoked Podcast — a workbook that mirrors the unique challenges and triumphs of Christian women navigating the

aftermath of divorce.

The UnYoked Approach:

The UnYoked philosophy, encapsulated within these pages, is not merely a

roadmap but a testament to the transformative power of faith. Grounded in

Christian principles, this workbook is crafted to guide you through the complex

terrain of emotions, offering a sanctuary for healing, self-discovery, and renewal.

Each chapter is carefully curated to address the multifaceted aspects of divorce

recovery, combining biblical wisdom, practical exercises, and a compassionate

understanding of the unique struggles faced by women.

Your Unique Journey:

One of the hallmarks of this workbook is its acknowledgment of the uniqueness

of your journey. Your story, emotions, and path to healing are unlike anyone

else's. This workbook does not seek to prescribe a one-size-fits-all solution but rather to provide a framework for self-reflection, growth, and restoration. Your

experience is valued, your pain acknowledged, and your resilience celebrated.

Embracing the Workbook:

As you embark on this journey through this workbook, consider it a sacred space

where vulnerability is met with compassion and growth is nurtured by faith. Each

chapter unfolds as a dialogue, encouraging you to reflect, pray, and engage with

the exercises in a way that feels authentic to your experience.

A Note of Gratitude:

Before you dive into the chapters that follow, I want to express my deepest

gratitude. Thank you for entrusting this workbook with your journey. It is my

sincerest hope that it becomes a source of strength, resilience, and unwavering

faith as you navigate the path of healing.

May these pages serve as a balm for your soul and a guiding light toward a

future filled with hope, purpose, and the unshakable knowledge that you are not

alone.

With heartfelt warmth,

Todd Turner

Chapter One

Dealing with Grief

"In the quiet corners of solitude, grief whispers it's somber melodies, echoing the ache of separation. Embracing the depths of sorrow, we find the courage to navigate the labyrinth of emotions, recognizing that within grief's embrace lies the transformative power to rebuild and rediscover yourself."

Grief is an intricate and often overwhelming emotion, a companion to the

profound changes brought about by divorce, by a life changing transformation. It

manifests in various forms and at unexpected times, leaving us grappling with the

enormity of our loss. In this chapter, we will explore the nature of grief,

understanding its facets, and navigating the path towards healing.

The Nature of Grief

Grief, in the context of divorce, is the emotional response to the loss of a shared

life, dreams, and companionship. It is not a linear process but a fluctuating

journey with different stages – denial, anger, bargaining, depression, and

acceptance. Understanding that grief is a multifaceted experience can help you

approach it with patience and self-compassion.

Processing Your New Reality

Accepting the reality of your changed circumstances is a crucial step in dealing

with grief. It involves acknowledging the loss, allowing yourself to feel the pain, and gradually adapting to the new normal. This can be tough because many

times our new normal has not even settled. But we can acknowledge that things

will not be "as they were."

Let's explore practical strategies to process these emotions and I will provide

some additional exercises at the end of this chapter.

- Journaling: Expressing your thoughts and feelings on paper can be a

    therapeutic outlet. Documenting your journey helps in gaining clarity,

    recognizing patterns, and tracking progress over time. As I say often,

    "Thoughts disentangle themselves over the lips and through the fingertips."

- Therapeutic Support: Seeking professional help from a therapist or

    Christian counselor provides a safe space to explore your emotions, gain

    insights, and develop coping mechanisms tailored to your specific

    situation. This is the "over the lips" part to disentangle your thoughts.

- Joining Support Groups: Connecting with others who share similar

    experiences through support groups or online forums fosters a sense of community and understanding. Sharing stories and insights can be

cathartic and reassuring. This very well may not be through your church.

More on this in the "church chapter" but chances are your church's small

group are not divorce recovery experts and might just offer some basic

"You should do more church" advice vs true recovery exercises.

Navigating Pain and Separation:

Pain is an inherent part of the grieving process and acknowledging it is vital for

healing. This pain can show up in many ways. I know I have had the curl up on

the bathroom floor and cry kind of pain. The sick-to-your-stomach, walking

around a grocery store pain. The "I just want the word to stop spinning" pain.

Mental anguish that turns into physical pain. This is common. This is normal. You

are not alone.

How can we navigate the pain associated with separation? Let's look at some

practical ways:

- **Self-Compassion**: Be gentle with yourself. Understand that healing takes time, and it's okay to feel a range of emotions. Practice self-compassion by treating yourself with the same kindness you would offer a friend. Your world may have turned upside down, you may "feel" like you have lost everything and hope is gone. That is just not true. But as you are in the pain, show yourself some love and kindness.

- **Establishing Boundaries**: Set healthy boundaries with your ex-spouse to protect your emotional well-being. Clearly define the terms of communication and interaction, allowing yourself the space needed for healing. This can be very hard with children involved. But avoiding triggers as much as possible and not engaging needlessly to pick fights, be right, or to dig would be very wise during this time.

- **Rediscovering Self-Identity**: Use this period of grief as an opportunity for self-discovery. Reconnect with your interests, invest time in personal growth, and redefine your identity beyond the constraints of your past relationship. I paused offering this advice right here. It is true but rest and recovery are the priorities but enjoying hobbies and putting a smile on your face doing things you love is great medicine.

Dealing with grief is an ongoing process that requires patience, self-reflection, and a commitment to personal healing. By understanding the nature of grief, processing your new reality, and navigating the pain associated with separation, you can embark on a journey toward renewal, self-discovery, and ultimately, a brighter future.

Some potential downsides you will want to avoid while grieving:

- **Don't feed your inner complainer** - Dwelling on your situation to anyone who speaks with you and having the internal conversations with yourself is not healthy. Complaining is a choice. Memorize Chuck Swindoll's famous quote "Life is 10% what happens to you and 90% how you respond.

- **Lack of Gratitude** - Cicero coined "Gratitude is not only the greatest of virtues but the parent of all the others." Removing this catalyst from your mindset can be very destructive to your recovery and to thriving again some day. Gratitude strengthens and enhances relationships and gives life and hope. Thank God for your blessings even when they sometimes feel they are evaporating quickly. We always have so much to thank our Lord for. Begin and end each day with thanks.

- **Listening to your inner-critic** - You must bring awareness to the tone and content of your self talk. We humans weigh negative thoughts at a much higher rate than positive thoughts and some of us have battered "self confidence," that has been walking around with the anchor of "belittling and criticism" from parents, loved ones, and even your past spouse. We start to believe and repeat. But we must remember we are a child of a King. Our worth is what He says it is. Not what broken people with their own agendas say it is.

The grieving that follows a divorce can be frequently compounded by the chatter in our minds and the chatter we allow out of our mouths. But saying "Just don't do that" really isn't sound or practical advice. Research actually says that trying to suppress thoughts, over long periods of time, actually increases thoughts. So let's learn to replace negative mindsets with more controlled thoughts and positive recovery tools that allow us to leave the fetal position and learn to fly… for some of you, for the first time ever.

To help you navigate this process, consider the following exercises:

Thanksgiving and Gratefulness:

Write down ten things you are thankful for:

That exists in your life.   That used to exist in your life.

_____   _____

_____   _____

_____   _____

_____   _____

_____   _____

_____   _____

Your Inner Voice Exposed:

Write down voices you tell yourself then truths from God's Word.

Your lies

(I'm not smart enough)

(I am not worthy of love)

_____

_____

_____

_____

_____

_____

God's Truths

(God made me for good works)

(God loves me as His own)

_____

_____

_____

_____

_____

_____

Blessings in The Storm

Write down your new situations and shift them into positives.

New Realities   **New Opportunities**

(I sold my home and live in a smaller space)   (I gained more time weekly for hobbies and exercise.)

(I sold my favorite car)   (I will save money on gas with my new car)

_____   _____

_____   _____

_____   _____

_____   _____

_____   _____

_____   _____

Listening to Your Body and Mind:

Write down what is happening to your body during your grieving time and these times of stress. Are there actions that can be taken to help you mitigate the negative effects on your body? (ie Very Tired… I could turn off Netflix at 9pm vs 2am. Weight gain… I could stress eat less and take more walks throughout the week.)

_____

Write down what comes out of your mouth throughout the day. Are there ways to replace complaining with acceptance, letting go, trusting God, and/or trusting yourself? (ie I spent an hour venting on a call today vs I took a step towards healing and moving forward.)

_____

Notice triggers and times of the day that cause negative attitudes or actions.

Identify spaces and moments you may need to fight or avoid. (ie Watching

Hallmark movies makes me feel sad and therefore I stress eat. Talking to my best friend gets me worked up.) Once identified, find replacement activities that will keep you from these triggers and try to switch and create new habits.

Observe a week and journal your findings and your new solutions.

Chapter Two

Losing Friends in a Divorce

"You are going to lose friends after divorce. It's a cold hard fact. Your life is

going to have some major transformations in the aftermath of UnYoking.

Let's navigate the delicate topic of losing friends during your transition,

offering perspectives, empathy, and strategies for building a new

supportive community. I have some ideas of how to salvage, strengthen,

and even release your friends."

Let's address the challenging truth first. The journey of divorce will inevitably lead to losing some friends – it's a tough reality. Some will distance themselves swiftly, others gradually. Your circle will change and these losses will hurt. The seismic impact of divorce reaches various aspects of our lives, with friendships being one of the affected corners. However, here's a silver lining. Ever wondered who your true friends are? Endure hardship and observe who stands by you. Proverbs 18:24 wisely tells us that a good friend sticks closer than a brother, and Proverbs 17:17 reminds us that a genuine friend loves at all times.

Divorce is painful on multiple fronts, including an often unspoken aspect as we navigate one of life's worst events. When we need our friends most, some start drifting away. Simple logistics may be a culprit – moving, changing jobs, relocating your child(ren) from a certain school, altering churches, or even leaving town. Financial constraints might also alter your lifestyle, making interactions awkward or even painful. Routines change and so do our abilities to engage with friends and friend groups.

Some friendships might dissolve due to people taking sides or avoiding making a choice, which, in itself, is a choice. If you were friends with a couple, the complexity deepens. We'll delve into this further... but let's begin with a significant loss: Our spouse.

Often, our spouse isn't just a life partner but also our confidant, our very best friend. The person with whom decisions were made during late-night conversations, hands held during road trips while discussing life goals and dreams, the coffee companion in the morning, starting the day together. The dissolution of a marriage not only ends the spousal connection but also severs the bond with a dear friend, causing pain and disrupting navigating life with a partner.

After a divorce, achieving some level of friendliness with an ex is possible, but for many, it's not that simple. If your divorce was mutual, agreed upon due to a fallen-apart marriage or irreconcilable differences, maintaining a friendship might be more feasible. However, most Christian divorces are not mutual; they often arise from tragedy. If one spouse perceives the marriage as fine and is blindsided by an affair or drastic lifestyle change leading to divorce, it's not just the loss of a spouse but of a "best friend." For those who discover their spouse cheating with one of your best friend(s), the loss is even more profound – a painful and brutal betrayal.

Losing our best friend and life partner is a harsh reality for many of us who've undergone divorce. Filling that emptiness overnight is unrealistic. Attempts to quickly date and replace that person can be challenging and sometimes fruitless.

Navigating post-divorce friendships can be truly exhausting. Our friend groups often diminish after a divorce, primarily due to fear and grief. Fear plays a significant role, as friends grapple with the unknown. They may feel uncertain about how to offer support during this challenging time, leading them to withdraw rather than communicate with you. The fear of doing or saying the wrong thing can

cause them to disappear from your life altogether.

Divorce becomes even more challenging for friends who were also close to your

ex-spouse. The dilemma of choosing sides becomes a real struggle for them.

Some opt not to choose at all, while others may take a side that is not yours.

There's a possibility they believe you mistreated your spouse and were at fault in

the marital issues. In such cases, they might align themselves with your ex-spouse.

Additionally, you may lose friends who were initially part of your spouse's social

circle.

Once the dust settles, it becomes evident who has drifted away and what decisions

were made by your friends. It can be surprising and somewhat painful. I recall

having a conversation with my ex, and as we reviewed our common friends, we discovered that none had taken a side. They had moved on from both of us. It was

a bit disheartening and even comical, but it's a part of the aftermath of separation.

Now, let's discuss the complexities of couple friendships. Your married or coupled

friends lose a friend after a divorce too – the friendship that was your marriage.

The breakdown of your marriage leaves them uncertain about how to navigate

these changed dynamics. Sometimes, it's because they can't see beyond their own

world and the relationships they've built for themselves. Sometimes its is because

it can be exhausting navigating the maze. The new reality of one couple being two

individual people may lead to awkward situations where they must choose sides

or segregate the friendship, with women bonding with women and men with men.

This often results in a convoluted web of "he said, she said" scenarios that they

would rather avoid navigating.

In essence, the aftermath of divorce impacts friendships in multifaceted ways. It's a process of understanding, acceptance, and, ultimately, finding a new equilibrium in our social circles. My marriage had three or four couples with whom we often hung out. The women continued their gatherings, leaving me feeling like the odd one out. As I frequently discuss on the UnYoked Podcast, men don't naturally form close-knit groups, we just don't tribe well. And honestly, I wasn't sure if they wanted me as their plus-one at events, and I didn't want to be that guy—the perpetual plus-one. It seems women fit into that role a bit more seamlessly. I went from spending multiple evenings a week with these friends to not hearing from any of them for over five years now. It's a strange phenomenon. Interestingly, I know a couple of women who play the plus-one role in couple groups for dinners, pool parties, and vacations. It just doesn't seem as much on the men's side. It's quite intriguing, right?

Some of you may encounter challenges in maintaining couple friendships due to societal perceptions and fears surrounding your newfound single status. The shift from being part of a couple, which is often considered off-limits and non-threatening, to being single can sometimes be perceived as a threat to the stability of their own marriages. There's even a term for this—"partner poaching." It's used to describe the fear some individuals have about their partners being attracted to or pursued by a newly single friend.

While this fear may seem a bit immature, it's more common than you might expect. It could explain why some couple friends have gone silent. They may not express it explicitly but it's a real concern. On the flip side, I know of a couple who intentionally chose to invest in one of the divorced singles. It wasn't random; they selected the one who needed the most help, love, and guidance. Instead of choosing the easy route, they opted for the person in greatest need. So, don't assume your friends will automatically pick you to maintain a friendship.

Some friends try to choose wisely, preferring to back the person doing things right, is the "most innocent," or is walking well with the Lord... not the one who had an affair or who just filed for divorce just "because I deserve to be happy." Your friends may feel better knowing they are supporting the "good person" and perhaps casting judgment on the one who made mistakes or a long line of unwise decisions. Admittedly, this perspective may seem a bit simplistic, but it happens more often than not... Pick the Honorable Side.

In reflecting on my own journey through divorce and now being single, I've gained valuable insights. When I encounter friends or couples going through a divorce, my approach has evolved. I strive to offer genuine friendship and support, especially to those navigating this challenging experience with kindness and wisdom, taking responsibility for their part in the mess.

I want to be there for individuals who find themselves in the midst of a difficult situation. Yet, I've also learned to "hold loosely" those who are justifying their foolish actions and giving up on their families. I've adopted a perspective akin to the parable of the prodigal son from the Bible. In that story, the father didn't chase after his wayward son but eagerly awaited his return, ready to embrace him with open arms when he repented. Similarly, I reach out, express love, and withhold judgment, allowing people the space to walk down their path. When they come to the realization that they've made mistakes, I'm there to support them—whether it's in rebuilding their marriage or assisting with their healing and coping with guilt.

My aim is not to brand someone with a metaphorical scarlet letter just because they walked away from a marriage. I've shifted away from the mindset of thinking, "Well, you made your bed, now lie in it," and excluding them from my life. I no longer see it that way. Every story has two sides, and I don't need to know all the details to extend love, check in, and be present for someone.

It's essential to recognize that true friends don't abandon you during times of crisis. However, people respond to tense situations differently and this divergence in coping mechanisms may lead friends or family members to distance themselves, leaving you to face hardships alone.

Here are some reasons why this might occur.

1. Choosing Sides:

Some friends may find themselves torn between supporting you or your ex-spouse, especially if they were friends with them first. It becomes a real challenge for them to maintain relationships with both parties.

2. Prioritizing Children:

If your children share common activities like attending the same school, playing together, or participating in church activities, parents often align themselves with the other parent for the sake of their children's needs. While maintaining a friendship with both parties might be ideal, it can lead to uncomfortable situations, pushing them to stand by the other parent.

3. Financial Challenges:

Assumptions about financial difficulties can strain relationships. When financial circumstances change due to divorce, the ability to participate in expensive social activities may diminish. Whether it's weekend golf outings or regular lunch or spa dates, exclusion from these events can occur naturally due to financial hardship or the perception of it.

4. Family Loyalty:

During your marriage, your spouse's extended family might have become your close friends. After a divorce, it's not typical for divorced couples to maintain strong relationships with their ex-spouse's family. Loyalty often takes precedence, and you might feel like you've lost a part of your family and close friendships that belonged to your ex-spouse. While some people remain close to their ex's family, it can be influenced by their guilt and a sense of justice, as they may feel your ex, their family member, was in the wrong.

In post-divorce life, understanding these dynamics and challenges can help navigate relationships with empathy and grace. It's okay to acknowledge the changes and, at times, the discomfort that may arise, as you forge a new path forward. Remember, everyone's journey is unique, and finding what works best for you is key to rebuilding and embracing a fulfilling life after divorce.

But remember, these reasons are not exhaustive, and individual circumstances vary 100%. It's essential to realize that people's reactions and choices in these challenging times will differ, affecting friendships. Post Divorce drama may run off some of your previous friends. Not all of your friends will know what to do and may simply retreat out of a protective nature over their own relationships. That's just the way it is.

Life is hard enough and divorce is messy. What friend has the time to navigate your new chaos consistently? It's your divorce, not your friend's divorce. So, many of them may run away. Be thankful for those who stay and for couples who work hard to keep you in their lives and friend groups. Losing friends is tough. I lost a lot—my career, my dad, my mom, my church, my town, my neighbors, all in a matter of a few years. The divorce was hard but my friend group's demise was super painful. Friends should be the one anchor you can count on during this crazy time. When they turn away and disappear, it's like another betrayal. It can really sting.

I think what many friends don't understand is that, as a divorcee, our world has turned upside down. Those stable friendships are anchors. Consistency in our lives is nice—not to be judged but to just stand beside me. I don't need my friends to hate my ex; I just want to know that my friends are there for me and want me in their lives when my world is on fire.

Research indicates that women experience a reduction of about 40% in their relationships following a divorce. I don't know where that number comes from; but, I did look it up. But women face a unique issue. Divorce can sometimes feel contagious to others. If a friend's marriage is unstable or going through difficulties, she may distance herself from you out of fear that her own marriage might end up in a very similar situation.

In addition to the concept of a social contagion, the lasting stigma surrounding divorce can also result in friends distancing themselves. Divorce is often viewed as a symbol of a failed marriage or a fractured family, carrying a sense of shame akin to wearing a giant scarlet letter. While this perception may have been more prevalent in the past, within the Christian community, there is still a tendency to

see divorce as a sign of giving up rather than displaying strength and endurance.

Moreover, many Christians regard married couples as part of the mainstream and

socially acceptable. Divorced individuals are sometimes perceived as belonging to

a different cultural group with more relaxed standards and morals. This distinction

creates a divide in how people perceive and relate to those who have gone through

divorce. Even without the stigma, it's important to note that friends often take sides,

not immediately but eventually. They choose to align with one spouse over the

other or neither spouse.

While this can lead to polarization, it is a common occurrence in divorce. As

humans, we naturally gravitate towards the status quo, the familiar, and the

reliable. Divorce disrupts all of that, effectively splitting relationships down the middle—literally. The previously established norm might have involved intact families sitting together at their children's soccer games, school events, and other places. However, divorce swiftly alters that structure, establishing a new normal. Divorced couples often find themselves on opposite sides of the park, opposite sides of the bleachers—physically and metaphorically.

This leaves many friends caught in the middle uncertain about how to navigate these new dynamics. Even in amicable divorces, there are still two opposing sides, and friends tend to align more strongly with one side over the other. Regardless of the reasons behind it, the feeling of abandonment by a close friend in a time of need can be incredibly hurtful. However, it's equally important to recognize and appreciate friends who share our values, can relate to our experiences, and show us empathy during these challenging times.

What can we do about this significant void in our lives as newly single Christians?

Let me share how I navigated this. I reset with a new friend group. I started over with a fresh set of friends.

So, let me share my story with you. There's a girl named Julie—yes, that's her real name. We first crossed paths on a dating app, you know how those things go. We chatted briefly, life took its course, and we both moved on. Then, after about a year, fate brought us back together. We matched again, and this time, we started having a daily conversation.

I remember saying, "Hey, I'm not even sure I have time for this. I don't know why I'm on this dating app. Well, actually, I do know why—I'm just a bit bored."

Despite our initial casual conversation, we soon realized we lived near each other. Julie seemed like a wonderful person, so we decided to meet up—but strictly as friends. We wanted to keep it simple and maintain a friendship.

We attended an outdoor jazz concert, soaking in the music and engaging in a delightful three-hour conversation. What made it special was the absence of any pressure to pursue a romantic relationship. In traditional dating, the focus tends to be on finding flaws that might signal a lack of compatibility. However, approaching it from a friendship perspective allows for a more relaxed experience.

When you're friends first, you appreciate a person for various qualities, and it's okay not to expect perfection. Everyone has quirks, unique laughs, or styles that might not align perfectly with your preferences. During those three hours, we savored each other's company without the need to scrutinize every detail.

As we left the concert, we realized how much we enjoyed this kind of simple, no-pressure interaction and wished we could do it more frequently, possibly with more people involved. That's when we decided to take action. We created two Bumble profiles, explicitly stating our intention for "co-ed friendship" only. The process, however, brought about some amusing and complicated moments.

I took on the task of curating a friends-only profile on the app, knowing that women would be viewing my profile. On the other hand, she did the same for men viewing her profile. The results were intriguing, with her receiving an overwhelming 700 swipes in just a week, while I got a more modest 17. It was a fascinating contrast, and we couldn't help but notice a possible reason behind it.

It became apparent that guys often swipe right on a pretty face, contributing to her high number of matches. Meanwhile, my profile, featuring pictures of us together and in group settings, left some women scratching their heads. It was an unexpected and somewhat awkward phenomenon that added a humorous twist to our experiment.

But with that said, we eventually gathered a big enough group of people to organize a breakfast. We all headed to a neighborhood taco shop, had breakfast, and met each other face-to-face. Over a year has passed since then, and we talk almost every day. We intentionally fostered these new friendships, and it turned out that we genuinely liked each other. We formed a strong bond, and I genuinely believe I'm true-friends with everyone in this group.

I've even taken some of them as plus ones to events like parties and concerts. Whenever someone needs a plus one, they simply reach out to the group. It's a true coed friend group, and it has been amazing because we share similar values and are in similar life situations. Importantly, we're not romantically involved with each other, which makes going out more cost-effective. As a guy, not always having to pay double for dates really makes a difference. It eliminates the emotional highs and lows of dating, allowing us to enjoy our time together without the pressure of dating.

Now, compare this with my church friends; they function a bit differently than the group I've formed. Church friends often suggest joining church singles groups, which can be a bit tricky.

Listen, I'm not willing to date someone from my church. I just don't want to. I don't want to have to avoid church services or events and have to dodge someone. The odds are it won't work out. I'm not ruling it out; I'm just saying the chances of finding a perfect match are slim. I prefer not to date within my church community. It's just awkward. And if it doesn't work out, well, then I might have to switch churches, making it even more problematic. What if that person likes me more than I like them? It puts everything into an uncomfortable situation. So, despite what people say about meeting someone in church, I'd rather not. I want to meet a Christian, just not from my church.

Now, you can find and make friends online in the dating pool. You might try to date someone, realize they're not your forever person, and still end up being friends. I've ended up with some amazing friends on the back side of a 1st date.

However, I know many people who, once they find out you're not their forever person, cut you out completely. They don't respond to your texts, they move on because they are dead serious about dating, and they don't know how to transition into being friends. I don't even know which approach is right or wrong. I see complexities in both ways. But I like to believe that if you meet someone who's a wonderful person but not your forever person, why wouldn't you stay friends with them? I just don't get it. But that's just me.

But don't let me romanticize becoming friends with the opposite sex. It has its problems and stigma.

There is the Harry Met Sally factor. Is it truly just a friendship? Does one side really have ulterior motives? Are they just long suffering their way into your arms one day?

There is the "date with a purpose" approach. Men hang with men. Women hang with women. And we ONLY interact for dating and marriage. And once we know we are not compatible in the marriage bond, then we have no reason to interact. I

think this mindset is born from the "purity culture" movement in America and really

can not be backed up scripturally, unless under the blanket of lust. But, what if…

just what if… we are not all animals and we can actually control our minds and

bodies and don't want or need to sleep with the opposite sex? Sounds crazy right?

That all men aren't dogs? Not all men are trying to bed every woman they interact

with?

I am friends with women. I have deep talks with many of them. I am here to say, it

can be done. And I am here to say, "I don't think God would condemn any of these

healthy, vibrant relationships.

But, I will acknowledge one potential caveat, your next boyfriend/husband… what

will he think? Well, as someone "next-husband one-day," I fully expect my new

wife will have dated and befriended men in the past. I am not marrying an 18 year

old virgin and I am not going to pretend that she was reading her Bible from the

day she signed her divorce papers or left her husband's funeral. The realities are that we are marrying someone for who they are; they ARE not who they WERE. I

just don't hold much concern for the purity optics of some Christian circles.

However, I 100% acknowledge that the day I wed my new bride, it will be much

easier to maintain my male friends than my female friends and my female friends

may fade away when they find their "next." It is just a reality and frankly, most likely

a wise and prudent reality.

Now, let me give you some tips as you navigate your friendships.

1) **Consider joining or creating a group via a dating app**. If you decide to

go for it, make it co-ed, its easier and a great way to meet a variety of

characters. I know someone who didn't make it co-ed; they loved the idea of

our friend group so much that they wanted to create their own, but only for

women. She had just moved to Dallas from another state and didn't know

anyone in town, so she decided to bring in just women. I understand it.

Maybe that's where you start – with a girls' friend group. Personally, I like the co-ed part. I don't want a group of guys just to do stereotypical guy things. I like the camaraderie and the conversations. I don't know; I just enjoy spending time with both women and men because the dynamics of a co-ed friend group are much cooler, and I've learned a lot along the way.

2) **Everyone also needs wise counsel.** If you lack wise people in your life, find one. It's not an easy task, and it may feel a bit insincere for me to suggest it's that simple. Seek some wise counsel. Some of you have had the opportunity but haven't taken it. Maybe you don't appreciate the voice of reason in your life. Perhaps you don't like being forced to face yourself when they speak the truth. Reach out to someone you know is speaking truth and being transparent, genuinely wanting the best for you. I count myself blessed to have six friends who are either pastors or former pastors. We regularly share meals and coffee, engaging in honest conversations. We poke, reveal, and pray for each other. I hold their words and friendships in high regard, so much so that I have a gold-framed photo collage of them in my office—a

daily reminder of the appreciation and value I place on their role in my life.

On the other hand, there's my college buddy group—friends with stories that could embarrass or even bury you if they got out. We exchange texts weekly, gather annually, attend each other's significant life events, and would go to great lengths for one another. Their unwavering support makes me feel truly loved. I also have a couple of other buddies who, while not pastors or college friends, have become important to me through deep connections and wisdom. Their authenticity and shared love for a good cigar and whiskey on the patio create a bond that goes beyond superficial connections.

Take a moment to appreciate the friends you have—those who stuck by you through both good and bad decisions. Consider writing them a note expressing your gratitude and acknowledging their value in your life. The Bible teaches that if one falls, another can help them up, emphasizing the importance of reliable friends who stick closer than brothers.

Lean into the trustworthy friends you have and express your gratitude. If there are old relationships that could be rekindled, maybe with a college roommate or an old work colleague, use technology, Facebook, and social media to your advantage. College alumni directories and other sources can help you reconnect.

If you find yourself in a post-divorce situation with friends offering poor advice, consider distancing yourself, even though it may be tough.

Remember not to isolate your friends, but instead, seek their company and give and receive sincere advice for each other's highest good. The Bible reminds us that a friend who sticks closer than a brother is a rare and valuable treasure. Navigating friendships after a divorce can be challenging, but here are some suggestions to help you on this journey. First and foremost, avoid making assumptions. Don't presume to understand other people's perspectives or motives without clear communication.

3) **Refrain from putting people on the spot or pressuring them to take sides.** This is crucial for maintaining healthy relationships, especially when it comes to couples. Instead, focus on finding birds of a feather—those who share similar values and interests. Remember, greater love involves self-sacrifice, so be willing to invest in others just as someone laid down their life for their friends.

4) **Give grace generously**, as mentioned in Proverbs 27:9: "Oil and perfume make the heart glad, but the sweetness of a friend comes from his earnest counsel." Be a source of comfort and wisdom to your friends, offering genuine support and advice.

To help you navigate this process, consider the following exercises:

Reflection Journaling:

Take time to reflect on friendships lost during or after your divorce. Write a letter to a friend you've lost, expressing your emotions, memories, and any unresolved feelings. Consider the impact of this friendship on your life. Whether you choose to mail the letter or not, write it as if they will be reading it. Start with writing down the top 5 characteristics you appreciate about him/her. Top 5 memories. Top five actions they have done to brighten your day or life. Then turn these lists into a letter.

Strengths and Values Inventory:

Identify your personal strengths and values that can contribute to building new friendships. Create a list and reflect on how these qualities can attract like-minded individuals. Think about ways to incorporate these strengths into your social interactions.

(I am a good people-connector. I am a great host for parties. I know a lot about Air

BnBs and travel hacks. I am the wittiest and funniest female west of the Ozarks.)

Community Vision Board:

Foster a positive outlook by creating a vision board representing the type of

community or friendships you desire. Include images, quotes, and symbols that

reflect supportive and uplifting relationships. This exercise can help you visualize

and manifest the positive connections you seek.

Friendship Affirmations:

Boost your confidence and self-worth in the process of making new connections.

Write down positive affirmations related to friendships and repeat them daily. This

practice will reinforce a positive mindset as you navigate new relationships.

(ie. Proverbs 16:28 A perverse person stirs up conflict, and a gossip separates close friends. Proverbs 18:24 One who has unreliable friends soon comes to ruin, but there is a friend who sticks closer than a brother. O. Henry "No friendship is an accident. ")

New Friendship Action Plan:

Develop a practical plan for meeting new people and building connections. Outline specific actions to take in the coming weeks and months, such as joining social groups, attending events, or volunteering. Set realistic goals and deadlines for initiating conversations and building connections.

1) Identify Friendships that are critical and valued.

2) What Actions can be taken to build and enhance?

3) Identify Friendships that are fractured or dormant.

4) What actions can be taken to mend fences or engage?

5) Identify new friendship possibilities that are yet to be known?

6) What action steps will kick start these new relationships?

Remember, the journey of rebuilding friendships post-divorce is an opportunity for personal growth and the formation of meaningful connections. Approach it with an open heart, give yourself the grace to learn and adapt, and trust that genuine friendships will blossom over time.

Chapter Three

Overcoming Isolation After Your Divorce

"Loneliness can be a powerful force post-divorce. Lonely apartments and quiet houses can be deafening to souls shattered by divorce. Let's delve into the depths of emotions, offering insights and strategies to overcome the challenges of solitude. It's time to transform loneliness into a journey of self-discovery and empowerment."

Some of us were merely roommates with our ex-spouses. Some were great co-parents, while others were more like business partners. Yet, for many of us, marriage meant having a best friend, a true life partner to navigate this world together. Someone to stand by us in tough times and share in the joys. There's a saying that goes, "Shared joy is double joy; shared sorrow is half sorrow."

Regardless of the depth of the relationship with your spouse, many of us have undoubtedly experienced profound loneliness post-divorce. A crushing loneliness as we find our way to being single and alone. Not just in the bedroom, not just at the kitchen table, not just while traveling, but in decision-making, life goals, and navigating the journey of life. It's incredibly and painfully challenging to grapple with this loneliness.

Let's delve into the struggles of being a lonely Christian single after a divorce. Let's begin with the harsh realities. Loneliness can lead us to some very dark places, and I can assure you that it can result in regrettable decisions. Simply attending church more frequently, joining a small group, or "Dating Jesus" will not solve certain types of lonely, for many it's not that simple.

The loneliness I want to address first isn't just about needing new friends or finding activities to keep us busy. It's about feeling truly alone when we don't want to be, as if all our options have vanished. Let me illustrate it this way: a few years ago, my dad passed away, right in the midst of my fight to save my marriage. My ex moved out just two days after my dad's funeral. Unfortunately, I didn't have the chance to properly mourn my father's death because a crisis superseded my grieving process.

After a few years, navigating a challenging battle with dementia, my mother passed away. It was a double-barrel grieving moment. Finally, I had time to sit with it. I missed my dad and mourned his loss. I missed my mom and mourned her loss. Unexpectedly, I mourned the loss of both my parents, feeling orphaned and alone in the world. There was no nest to fly back to in times of trouble, no phone call home for advice or to share joy.

This realization hit me when I lost my wife, my best friend, and my kids were reaching the age of leaving the nest. They were flying out into their own lives, leaving me with a huge void and forcing me to confront my grief. I experienced profound loneliness, a feeling I struggle to describe. Even now, I'm in therapy, grappling with the depth of that experience.

This level of solitude couldn't be fixed with a card night on Tuesdays or volunteering for the youth program at church. For those of us Unyoked, the shattering of routines, realities, and the absence of your life partner can bring real moments of pain.

It's a loneliness stemming from the harsh reality that everything you once knew is gone and can't be restored. It's a blending of mourning and boredom. When the grip of loneliness tightens, your mind can wander down treacherous paths. Thoughts of a lifetime of solitude may haunt you, fueled by a long list of perceived flaws. This downward spiral of misery can be hard to break free from.

I want to assure you that many going through a divorce experiences gut-wrenching loneliness. (Some may even have encountered this loneliness while still in their marriages, long before the decision to divorce… which can lead to immersing themselves in activities like affairs or drinking… numbing… to distract from the pain.)

For parents of active children, staying busy and engaged can help illuminate the "quietness or boredom" that leads to loneliness. But anger towards an ex-spouse often fills the time as bitterness begins to creep in the heart.

Loneliness is a natural part of the healing process after a divorce. It's like a companion to grief, bidding farewell to so much, including that feeling of belonging that makes you wonder if you'll ever experience it again. There are triggers for loneliness that linger until addressed or time passes … like yard work, taking out the trash, or making the bed alone. Many women I've spoken to mention feeling lonely while pumping gas, managing bills, cooking certain meals, grocery shopping, and during holidays or travel. These are the things your partner used to do or help with or traditions your family once held. They serve as reminders, sometimes painful, sometimes just gentle nudges that you're now on your own.

For those who missed the UnYoked "Church Episode," we discussed a strange catch-22. We often feel that the one place where we should feel accepted and valued—the church—is the same place where we feel the least heard and valued. It's a true shame. Losing friends adds another layer of loneliness, as people we once relied on fade away. But let's be fair. In the beginning, you might have sought solace in isolation as a way to cope with the intense pain from the end of your marriage. Perhaps you tried to find comfort in the company of existing friends, those you knew before the divorce. Seeking such protection after such a significant life event is natural.

However, you may now find yourself facing a different challenge. While the pain persists, you no longer feel a sense of belonging with those friends. Instead, you sense a growing distance—a feeling of being different from them. You know that feeling of being alone in a group, right? Yeah, we may all be together, but you guys get to go home and snuggle. You guys get to go home and do life together. I'm going home… alone again.

A possible reason for the disconnect is that they're married; you're not. Your life and circumstances have changed, and you no longer fit as seamlessly as you once did. This isn't necessarily due to any action on their part, but rather a consequence of your transformed identity after divorce.

I remember once getting mad at being alone. I had to get up and go use the restroom in the middle of the night. I looked over at the empty side of the bed and flung off the blanket, with anger…. Not sure how to describe being angry and taking it out on a sheet and blanket… but it happened. :) I popped right up. I was upset that I was alone. I was mad that I was sleeping alone. I was frustrated that I felt

forced into this new situation. I wanted somebody to talk to. I wanted somebody I

had to be quiet for when I went to the restroom. I wanted somebody I could cuddle

up next to, when I got back in bed. All that familiarity was gone and I didn't like it

at all.

Now, with time, you come to terms with the reality that your life as a suddenly

single person is distinct from that of a married individual. If you can't have that

person in your life, you may yearn for someone who can truly comprehend the

complexities of your new life. There are numerous individuals who deeply

understand what you're going through. They are fellow "suddenly single" people.

We're out here; we're an army. And no, I'm not suggesting diving into the dating

scene. I'm talking about making genuine friendships.

Dating might not be the best idea at the moment, so let's delve into that. Many of

you reading might find yourselves struggling with codependency. After going

through divorces, it's common to experience a significant dip in self-esteem, and unfortunately, some may even grapple with depression and PTSD. Codependency often shares traits with a healthy desire for "human connection" and I'd like to shed light on that. If you think you might be codependent? I want you to take a quick quiz from my friend Harmony Dust, the writer of the forward of this workbook. Codependency is a widespread, often unseen condition that wreaks havoc in people's lives and relationships. If you have ever wondered if you struggle with codependency, Harmony and her team created this 3-minute quiz for you! Use

QR Code to Access

Until these traits are addressed and resolved, engaging in dating might not be the

best course of action. Dating can potentially create more problems than it solves.

It's essential to focus on personal growth and overcoming codependency before venturing into new relationships.

Dating before being healed seems similar to a drug addict who believes the next hit will solve their problems, but in reality, it only makes things worse. A new boyfriend/girlfriend may have some highs and good feelings but can take you off the path of healing. You can have friends of the opposite sex if you're considering dating, but don't assume your issues will disappear when you find someone to fill your time, sit on the couch with you, and share a dinner. We are social animals and we need friends, but it is important to choose wisely.

This reminds me of a joke about a guy who moved into the wilderness. After months of isolation, he spotted another man in the distance pulling a mule. They finally met in the middle and the first guy expressed his loneliness and was so happy to finally see another soul. The other guy invited him to his upcoming party with fighting, gambling, and drinking. Excited, the first guy asked when everyone would arrive, only to find out it was just going to be "the two of them." The point is, people need people in their lives and sometimes they'll tolerate anything just to have somebody around.

Whether you are codependent, lonely, bored or just a social animal, your next step should always be "wholeness." What does that even look like? Well it starts with forgiveness. Self forgiveness. Healthy grieving (Maybe you need to revisit the exercises listed at the end of chapter 1?) Owning your faults and parts in your divorce and in the aftermath of the UnYoking process. Looking at patterns in your relationship choices and digging into the people and situations you attract.

Healthy attracts healthy. Broken attracts broken. If you are looking for a friend or a partner, you MUST be healed to attract quality people in your life.

But who should be your friends? The answer depends on your stage of life. If you have young kids, it's beneficial to connect with people who align with your children's activities—lawn chairs, bleacher seats, tryouts, practices, recitals, and games. In the empty nest phase of life or for parents sharing custody 50-50, finding the right companionship becomes crucial.

Some of you excel in parenting during 50% of your time and then navigating the challenges of loneliness during the other half. It's a tough roller coaster ride and my heart breaks for those facing such situations. For those with zero or limited custody of their kids, I acknowledge the eeriness of a quiet house—it can be a deeply painful experience.

I understand the challenge firsthand. There was a time when I had custody of my kids and I managed our vacation/holiday schedules. During one Christmas, I thought it would be best for the kids to spend the morning with my ex-wife and her parents. My own parents had passed away and I wanted my kids to experience the joy of traditional Christmas morning with their "other family." So, I sat on the couch alone on Christmas day. That day stands out as one of the worst in my life, ranking in the top three for sure. I felt an indescribable loneliness, a loneliness that couldn't be fixed because what could I do? It was Christmas and a Sunday, and everything seemed closed. Though some friends later said I should have called them, I found myself in a real and unfixable situation. While their offers of companionship were kind, sometimes people's presence doesn't alleviate our pain. Watching another family open presents would have been weird for everyone but I appreciated their concern.

I've experienced female friends asking for hugs or companionship, seeking some comfort from their feelings. On at least two occasions, two separate female friends reached out for a simple hug or to cuddle or even to take a nap together. They were lonely and crave companionship and even simple human touch. Maybe even just to feel the warmth of protection and safety. These instances reflected a deep loneliness, a yearning for security and touch. When we unyoke and become more independent and in charge of our own security and happiness, the solitude can become overwhelming. The craving for stability and comfort can be a huge draw for us in times of quiet and frustration.

In the insightful book, "The Body Keeps Score," the impact of stress on our lives takes center stage, shedding light on the profound connection between our emotions and physical well-being. As we navigate through stress and depression, our bodies undergo transformative changes. This book serves as a valuable resource, offering a deeper understanding of this intricate relationship.

Contrary to the belief that dating is exclusively reserved for marriage, there's a therapeutic aspect to it that shouldn't be overlooked. Engaging in meaningful conversations and spending time with others can be a powerful exercise. While some argue that dating for reasons other than marriage might be a waste of time, the reality is that these interactions can be profoundly therapeutic.

Breaking free from the shackles of loneliness, even if it means going on casual dates, can be a significant win. It might not align with traditional "church" views on dating, but the positive impact on one's well-being or sanity cannot be ignored. For some women, a night out may simply be about enjoying a meal and a rewarding conversation. While it may seem like a trivial pursuit to some, these outings can be a therapeutic and soul-nourishing experience. This approach to dating without a "marriage approach" might be too much to swallow for some of you. Even fraternizing with "the other gender" for a friendship might ruffle feathers: yours, your families, friends, or your church. As I mentioned before, I do not see the warning in scripture about making friends of the opposite sex. Do not confuse warnings on lust with a command to not get near the opposite sex. This is as irrational as "don't dance because it might lead to sex" or "don't drink because it leads to drunkenness." They are illogical leaps and not Biblical at all. Prudency and modesty.. Sure. Of course. But abstinence and deprivation of rewarding, colorful, life-giving personalities and situations…. No. Life is full of wonderful opportunities and people and our prudent, rule-enforcing, simplistic guardrails might be limiting friendships and opportunities for you in this next phase of life.

However, seeking companionship out of loneliness carries its own set of risks and vulnerabilities. Many find themselves falling into the trap of rushing into new relationships as a means to cope with the void left by divorce. This can have tragic consequences, as entering into a new relationship without allowing time for complete healing may lead to repeating patterns with someone similar to our ex-partner or someone entirely different.

In conclusion, the journey of seeking companionship and navigating relationships requires a delicate balance. While the benefits of casual dating are debatable, it's crucial to be mindful of the risks involved. Taking the time to heal and become whole individuals again is paramount to avoiding the pitfalls of repeating past mistakes. By understanding the complexities of dating and relationships, we can embark on a journey towards genuine healing and fulfillment.

The Next Break Up

In many instances, the aftermath of a breakup can be challenging, and I can personally attest to the emotional toll of parting ways with a new partner while still recovering from my divorce. It felt like a double blow, making me feel like a loser all over again. Time and the waiting game are generally your best bed fellows during this time, pun intended.

Making Your Children Your Friends

Sadly, some parents resort to discussing their loneliness with their children after a divorce, thinking they are "just being honest" and seeking a connection with their child. However, this approach can needlessly burden their child with adult concerns and I firmly believe that children should never be placed in a position of being their parents' friend during a divorce. The long-term effects on both the kids and the parent-child relationship can be incredibly damaging. Your kid(s) need a parent and stability more than they need authenticity during this time, most likely.

Fighting That Feeling

It is crucial to find someone else to confide in and share your struggles with. Understanding that loneliness is a natural part of the divorce recovery process is essential. Instead of fighting against it, I encourage you to embrace it as a necessary step in your journey. By accepting and acknowledging your loneliness, you can navigate through it—perhaps quickly, perhaps not—but definitely effectively.

Suppose you're ready to stop fighting and numbing and embrace this part of the divorce recovery process. In that case, I have some assignments that can help you cope with loneliness more effectively, such as setting healthy boundaries and establishing new relationships.

A dear friend of mine describes those moments of intense loneliness as "kitchen floor moments" when you find yourself in anguish, wrestling with God, and just laying on the kitchen floor. It's okay to feel lonely; it's okay to hurt. However, seeking a quick fix with a new relationship may not be wise.

Here are some valuable steps to help you overcome loneliness after divorce:

1. **Connect with Loved Ones:** Strengthen your existing relationships. Reach out to family members, distant cousins, and close friends who can provide love, support, and understanding. Strengthening these connections, which may have wavered during busy seasons of life, can help alleviate loneliness and provide a sense of belonging.

2. **Zoom Dates and Online Friendships:** Online friendships can be a great first step. Zoom has changed how we interact with our community. People can host happy hours online and you don't have to get "going out ready." Just put your hair in a ponytail or throw on a T-shirt, and connect on Zoom. Talking to somebody is not that hard; you don't even have to leave the house.

3. **Force Yourself to Be Social:** Exercise those social muscles. It's okay to take baby steps—go sit in the back, arrive late, leave early. Even if you have to drive to an event's door and turn around, that's fine. Make efforts to engage in social activities, attend gatherings, join clubs or groups aligned with your interests, and participate in community events. Pushing yourself to interact with others can open new doors to friendships and possibilities.

Remember, it's perfectly fine to take things one step at a time. I have a friend who excels at walking into a room and finding those who need someone to talk to—

baby steps and sitting in the corner with others who may feel the same way can make a big difference.

One time in Israel, our group found ourselves in Jerusalem at the world renowned holocaust museum. Amidst the hustle and bustle, a little lady caught a few of our attention, she was walking alone struggling to keep up with the pace of the crowds. I must confess, caught up in my own world, chatting away with someone, I likely walked right past her. Similarly, my friend, just as busy as me, noticed this lady and chose to approach and walk with her. It turned out she was a Holocaust survivor. He accompanied her through the entire Holocaust museum, absorbing her stories. "There's my family," she'd say, pointing, "there's my sister," reliving the past. This simple act of attentiveness led to a profound connection and a rich experience. He found the person in the room who needed help. Who stood apart. He reached out and was deeply rewarded.

Consider this: in almost every room, there's likely someone who, like you, may not want to be there, had a tough day, or is likely going through something. A little attentiveness can go a long way, perhaps leading to a reciprocal connection.

Look around. Not everyone is having a good time; there are others struggling, just like you.

Here are some practical steps to enhance your well-being:

1. **Engage in Volunteer Work**: Volunteering not only benefits others but also provides a sense of purpose and fulfillment. It can help shift your focus from personal struggles to making a positive impact in the lives of others. Creating a sense of connection and fulfillment, helping someone in need might reveal how blessed you truly are.

2. **Rediscover Your Passions**: Reconnect with activities that may have taken a backseat during marriage or child-rearing years. Engage in hobbies that bring you fulfillment and renew your sense of self. Whether it's painting, dancing, singing, working out, or writing, try something you enjoy, perhaps even in a class setting, alone but in public.

3. **Limit Social Media Use**: While social media can be a useful tool for connecting, it can also contribute to feelings of loneliness and comparison. Take breaks from social media platforms and focus on nurturing real-life connections

and experiences. Remember, social media can make you feel lonely and inadequate.

4. **Establish a Daily Routine**: Work on yourself by creating a daily routine that includes self-care activities such as exercise, meditation, journaling, and personal goal setting. Prioritize self-improvement and personal growth to boost your confidence, self-esteem, and overall well-being.

5. **Know the Difference Between Feeling Lonely and Being Alone**: Allow yourself to feel sad when necessary, but avoid dwelling in misery. Recognize that there is a distinction between feeling lonely and being alone. Embrace solitude when needed, appreciating the opportunity for self-reflection and personal growth.

By implementing these steps, you can navigate through feelings of loneliness and embark on a journey towards self-discovery and fulfillment.

It's crucial to recognize and process your emotions after divorce. Give yourself the space to grieve, but actively focus on healing and moving forward. Look for healthy ways to express your emotions, such as through therapy, support groups, or confiding in a trusted friend. Seeking professional help from a therapist, counselor, or divorce coach specializing in post-divorce support can provide valuable tools and coping strategies. They offer a safe space to explore your feelings, helping you overcome loneliness and find a path to healing.

Remember, healing takes time, and everyone's journey is unique. Be patient with yourself, practice self-compassion, and understand that, with support and self-care, you can rebuild a fulfilling and meaningful life beyond your untying. I'm uncertain about the balance between isolation and loneliness, but I firmly believe in the saying, "You can't run a marathon, then take a nap." Be cautious about the self-care valley potentially leading to isolation or even depression if not managed properly.

Helpful Exercises

Loneliness Journaling:

Exercise: Keep a loneliness journal for a week. Write about moments of solitude, emotions experienced, and any patterns noticed. Reflect on the sources of loneliness and consider how they can be addressed.

Creating a Comfort List:

List activities, hobbies, or practices that bring a sense of comfort. Create a personalized comfort list and commit to incorporating at least one comforting activity into each day.

What do I enjoy doing?

What skill sets do I possess that bring me joy?

What hobbies do/did I enjoy and what hobbies might I want to pursue?

Self-Discovery Letter:

Write a letter to yourself exploring the positive aspects of being alone. Plan to read this letter in 3 months. Focus on self-discovery, personal growth, and newfound strengths. Highlight how you can transform loneliness into an opportunity for empowerment. You can look back and be so proud of today's version of you for empowering your future self.

Connection Map:

Create a connection map by listing friends, family, or acquaintances who have been supportive. Consider reaching out to one person on the list each week, whether through a call, message, or a planned meeting. Always lay a piece of wood on your friendship fire to keep it burning.

Vision for the Future:

Write a vision statement for the future, describing the type of connections and relationships desired. Outline small steps that can be taken today to move towards that vision, fostering hope and motivation.

Chapter Four

The Church and The Divorce Dilemma

"Your church may have let you down during and after your divorce. Many

do. Did you feel ostracized, abandoned, and perhaps even betrayed?

Explore the often-unspoken struggles faced by those who bear the scarlet

letter of divorce while sitting in the church pews. Learn how to strike a

balance between poor advice and extending grace amidst the complexities

of navigating the church."

This chapter holds a unique resonance compared to others. It may stir some

controversy, as it aims to prompt introspection. My sincere prayer is that this

chapter achieves two crucial objectives. Firstly, it articulates the thoughts and

experiences of Christian divorcees navigating broken systems within today's

American churches. Secondly, I hope it sheds light on church leaders who may be willing to step outside traditions and comfort zones to minister more effectively to those affected by divorce—statistics reveal this includes anywhere between 40 and 50% of church members.

At the time of writing this book, I have been divorced for over five years. I've encountered only a small handful of divorcees who haven't been scarred, hurt, or frustrated with their churches post-divorce. The reality is that most church leaders assume couples have simply "drifted away" from their flocks post-divorce, oblivious to the fact that their programs, words from the pulpit, or lack of empathy might have driven people away. This has proven true more often than not.

In this workbook, we'll delve into the challenges faced by the American church and the divorcee… Church: When the solution hurts.

Allow me to insert a disclaimer right at the beginning. I recognize that there may

be readers unfamiliar with me or the Unyoked podcast, and they might think I

romanticize divorce or don't take Scripture seriously. Neither is true. The Unyoked

podcast was not created to dissect the intricacies of God's view on marriage or

divorce. Numerous sermons already exist that break down a Genesis view of God's

perfect plan for marriage. Instead, my podcast and writings speak to those living

in a broken world, attempting to navigate a challenging road. We discuss emotions,

not just ideal theology. I tackle subjects rarely heard from a pulpit, hoping Christian

leaders gain a new perspective on the people in their flock, their mindset, and their

obstacles. And I hope to equip and empathize with fellow divorcees.

I'm aware that some may approach this content with a judgmental lens, questioning

if it aligns with "truth theology." However, I urge everyone to remember that Jesus

embodied both mercy and truth. I ask anyone reading this to don a lens of empathy

and mercy while retaining their truth lens. That's all I can request. Remember Job's

friends? They began well, coming to their friend in a time of need, sitting with him in silence. But when they opened their mouths, it all went downhill. They shared

their opinions, asked the wrong questions, and made assumptions. Divorce is a

profoundly traumatic event in people's lives. When we're brought to our knees,

some Christians may falter as theologians and as makeshift ministers.

Let's begin by addressing the spoken and unspoken stigma of divorce.

In Christianity, God holds marriage in high regard, and it's crucial for us to share

this perspective. Safeguarding the sanctity of marriage is essential, but let's be

clear—it doesn't mean blindly defending it "at all costs." If a situation involves

bodily harm, like a man abusing his wife during nights of drinking, the priority is not

to protect such a marriage. Instead, the focus should shift to safeguarding the well-

being of the wife and her children.

Misunderstandings arise when some preachers insist on preserving marriage

without acknowledging valid reasons for divorce that align with God's will or even

God's allowance. Divorce is permissible in various cases, and as Christians, we must recognize situations where it becomes necessary to ensure the safety and health of individuals, including their mental well-being. Yep, I said it.

While our pulpits stress the significance of upholding marriage, they often touch on issues like affairs or abuse as grounds for divorce. However, there's a need to delve deeper into less-discussed matters. The Bible and many pastors might not provide explicit guidance on topics like mental illness, different forms of abuse (verbal, mental, financial), struggles with alcoholism or drug use, various types of child abuse, sexual abstinence, the challenge of keeping a marriage facade while not truly acting married, and the complexities of living separately.

Many of us have faced sleepless nights, grappling with tough situations and decisions, only to find sermons primarily focused on Genesis 1 and 2, offering little practical advice for the messy, real-world situations we navigate.

The Scarlet Letter "D"

Let's address the issue of stigma. Passing judgment on divorce decisions, whether it's from pastors, church leadership, or small groups, creates an unwelcoming atmosphere for those of us who have encountered challenging issues. Even in grace-filled, loving, Christ-centered churches, divorced individuals often feel marked with an undeniable sense of judgment as they walk in.

Consider this scenario: Picture yourself in a massive car wreck—bloodied, clothes torn, limping—and entering a church where everyone greets you with smiles, behaving as if everything is normal. However, it's far from normal. You're in pain, visibly injured by a massive wreck. Similarly, divorced individuals have undergone a significant tragedy, feeling gutted, bruised, often embarrassed, hurt, and judged. Meanwhile, the sermon addresses how cars shouldn't get into wrecks, as they aren't designed for that. While we acknowledge the truth in the pastor's words, where is the mercy? We've been through a wreck; why aren't we discussing it? Why must we sit here and absorb the truth without the accompanying mercy?

Let's move beyond the theoretical aspects of a perfect marriage and delve into the real issues that we navigate in a broken world. We are truly divorced and we are genuinely crushed. Metaphorically, our cars have been wrecked. Now what?

There's often an undertone of "your marriage failed," and for those of us whose marriages didn't last, does the church think less of me, less of my spouse, less of both of us for the mistakes that led to our divorce? Frequently, there are many underlying issues in a divorce. Oftentimes, the publicly stated reason for the divorce is not even the real reason.

Now for some of us, our ex-spouses still attend the same church or participate in church events just as we do. Every awkward interaction serves as a reminder of our new divorced reality. As we navigate conversations that either ignore our unusual circumstances or address them awkwardly, we feel compelled to explain things, unsure of which details to reveal and which ones to withhold. It's much easier to simply avoid the situation, which is one of the reasons we choose not to attend. Sitting together is not an option and sitting apart feels strange.

Here's another way the divorce stigma manifests itself: in family-centered churches that openly market and cater to "family first." There have been numerous books on this topic and some may question, "What's wrong with that? The Bible is pro-family." While that is true, if you examine the New Testament teachings and prioritize them, the emphasis on family has been at the expense of creating space for members of the body of Christ that do not conform to the traditional family. 2.5 kids and a dog. This "family" emphasis excludes singles, widowers, divorced families, single parents by choice, foster and adoptive families. "Family First" has become a defining characteristic of many churches in America. Contrary to the Bible, which does not prioritize families over individuals, many churches, marketing strategies, and event planners assume otherwise. In fact, in the Bible, Paul implies that marriage and family may be a less desired route to take. Despite this, not only do we not celebrate being single, but we also often assume it to be sub-standard.

I once stopped attending a Sunday School class because every announcement assumed "childcare and spouses and families" and there was a lack of even considering a person, who wanted to attend an event, just might be single. i.e. The fee is $40 per couple. Childcare included. Bring 3 cans of food for donation. Is it $20 for me... and 1.5 cans of food? The church often feels unwelcoming because many events and much of the marketing is built around a family-oriented tone. I know of churches that have asked worship team members to step back or stand at the back of the stage while navigating divorce, as if divorce is not just a marriage failure but a personal failure. Or that divorced or divorcing members can't possibly worship or lead worship.

There's a church near me that takes a strong stance on the issue of divorce and remarriage, swinging the pendulum in a rather strict direction. They require individuals who have gone through divorce to make efforts towards reconciliation with their ex-spouse before the church will approve or sanctify their new relationships or marriages. Additionally, a public apology for sins committed in the previous marriage is mandatory, to be delivered in front of the congregation before church membership or remarriage is permitted.

Curiously, there seems to be a lack of public apologies for other sins such as obesity, pornography consumption, addiction, tax fraud, jealousy, lying, and gossip – to name a few. It's perplexing that only divorced individuals are subjected to public "confession" on stage. Talk about the Scarlet Letter "D."

I know of a man who was once part of a church staff. When his long-time ex-wife expressed a desire to possibly restore their marriage, she informed the elders, leading to their insistence that he take a sabbatical leave to consider the possibility. Reluctantly, he complied, only to vehemently reject the idea upon further reflection. Since when is it within the elders' purview to mandate such decisions? Once again, this mindset to "maintain a marriage" appears to be a prioritization of "truth over mercy." While acknowledging the importance of marriage, the lack of mercy in this situation is glaring. Disregarding the pain and anguish caused by his ex wife's affairs and her constant deceit, the pressure to force restoration seems highly inappropriate. The man has moved on, is now single, and it is not the elders' responsibility to guide him based on their perception of "God wants you two to remarry."

Often divorcees feel unfairly singled out, pun intended.

Now, let's delve deeper into the dynamics of ministering to single individuals, particularly from the pulpit.

Christians across the nation often witness pastors speaking without truly delving into God's Word, merely stringing together verses to serve their sermon's purpose. This practice has its major consequences and it's crucial that we understand how this trend ripples into our lives. So, how do pastors and their sermons relate to divorce and divorce care? Well, most of us who are listening have a male, married pastor who has never experienced divorce. His sermons are limited in scope and knowledge. Therefore, seeking relevant information about our divorce journey from him is akin to asking a teenage boy what it's like to be pregnant. So, what usually occurs is a 40-minute sermon at best, covering "Here's what the Bible says about marriage and here's what the Bible says about divorce," with a somewhat idealistic message about God's perfect plan for marriage. While God values marriage, there is almost silence on mercy, which He highly values as well. What is lacking is guidance on how to love someone amidst the turmoil of a broken marriage and a shattered family and assistance in navigating the landmines of divorce.

This gap in ministering and speaking to divorcees led to the creation of this workbook and my UnYoked Podcast. I wanted to address "The Pain, Process, and Possibilities post a Christian Divorce." Divorce and the new single life are challenging and American Christian culture doesn't make navigating decisions and dealing with the ripple effects of divorce any easier. While Christian marriage and divorce advice abound, they often conflict with the harsh realities of pain, abuse, and loneliness in the real world.

God communicates more than just "I hate divorce." He establishes a standard that, despite not always being met, He graciously works to restore and renew individuals. For those of us navigating the profound experience of parting ways with a spouse or upheaving a family, the journey often takes us through dark, lonely, and confusing places. Unfortunately, our challenges are seldom addressed from the pulpit, and the advice received may not always align with our unique circumstances.

I want to create a space where divorced women can safely grapple with the tension between God's plan and the harsh realities of living in a broken world filled with broken people and fractured relationships.

As a Christian, I've observed a significant gap in divorce care within our churches, and I've felt compelled to address it, even in a modest way.

The challenges we face as divorcees are often exacerbated when pastors, with limited experience in complex issues and counseling, become our primary source of guidance. In our quest for support, we can and should often turn to friends, support groups, books, podcasts, or individuals who can truly empathize with our needs, experiences, and emotions. While our church's small groups may provide a sense of community, it's important to acknowledge that they may not always offer the specialized assistance required for navigating the intricacies of divorce and its ripple effects.

As discussed, many church groups often lack individuals with the qualifications to guide us through the complexities of divorce. Their understanding typically mirrors that of their pastor, limiting their ability to provide comprehensive assistance in post-divorce situations. While they may offer warmth and compassion to a soul weathering the storm of divorce, their advice on dating, reconciliation attempts, constant church event invitations, and more may not address the profound challenges we face or feel relevant.

In the midst of these profound life changes, it can be overwhelming when well-meaning individuals suggest "volunteering at church, preparing casseroles for small groups, or assisting with various church activities." While these gestures are undoubtedly well-intentioned, it's essential to consider whether investing our time in these pursuits is genuinely beneficial when compared to addressing the crises we are currently facing in our lives.

As we seek support and understanding during the turbulent journey of post-divorce life, it's essential to look beyond the traditional avenues provided by the church. Exploring resources that cater to the specific challenges we encounter can assist us as we search to find solace, guidance, and practical solutions as we navigate this intricate chapter of our lives.

A divorce is more than just a decision; it involves negotiating a settlement, moving out, and moving forward with our lives. The demands of many American churches may not be a top priority for those facing real challenges in their new circumstances.

For individuals in crisis, consider the analogy of being a victim of a natural disaster. In such times, genuine, life saving help is critical — shelter, food, water, clothing, transportation, and the means to restore utilities. Imagine the Red Cross approaching a victim and instead of giving them what they need... they ask for them to volunteer but also to organize a donation drive, or to ensure everyone wears red shirts, or to make a van look great for the next disaster. In such a scenario, you might find it hard not to roll your eyes while you realize, "This is what churches do—asking people in crisis to contribute to the busy church machine while they are dealing with their own crises." It's almost comical and it certainly is short sighted.

The disparity between the urgent needs of those in crisis and the church's priorities becomes apparent. Ministry focus should be on providing genuine support and understanding to those navigating difficult times, rather than burdening them with additional responsibilities.

How churches align with God's vision of "loving your neighbor and caring for widows and orphans" has a lot to do with how they "minister to" vs "preach towards" those in need. While I won't delve too deeply into this tangent, it significantly influences how churches minister to those experiencing divorce. The assumption that "conversions to Christianity" primarily occur within church walls has led many American churches to often prioritize "the wow factor" - the spectacle, the sermon, and the satisfaction of attendees and sometimes they neglect the needs of hurting believers and members. Church is for members. The gospel is for those on the out. American churches often get this wrong and it's members frequently suffer.

Now, let's shift our focus to the behind-the-scenes aspects, not the ones on the "church stage" but those in the hallways. A phrase that is often aimed at divorcees from fellow Christians or church staff is "Date Jesus." I understand the sentiment— it's a vague expression meant to convey that Jesus is the ultimate solution. The idea is that when you're in need, Jesus is ever-present for you. It also implies that, instead of dwelling on the absence of your spouse or succumbing to suffering, you should invest that time in the Word and deepen your relationship with Christ.

However, here lies the issue with this vague and superficial advice: it's just that— vague and superficial. It's comparable to telling someone facing unemployment, impending utility shutoffs, and the threat of car repossession, "Hey, you should start your own business." While true, it might not be the most applicable advice at that moment. It's akin to advising a hungry child in Ethiopia, "You should dig a well and cultivate your own crops." While valid, it will not address the real immediate need. When we find ourselves lonely, crushed, perhaps even battling depression amid a storm of issues, receiving vague suggestions that don't address our current needs and situations can feel disengaged and insensitive.

A few weeks after my divorce, a friend dropped by for a visit. Like Job's friend, his intentions were good, but what he said caught me off guard. He said "My wife and I were discussing divorce and death the other day and we decided that if we ever lost each other, instead of remarrying, we would commit our lives to the church and serve Jesus." My expression must have spoken volumes. It felt a lot like telling

a starving kid in Ethiopia, "If I were in your situation, I'd use my hunger to spread

the gospel to other hungry people because I'm that spiritual. I'd probably Date

Jesus, too, while digging a well." It was the wrong thing to say at that moment and

had me rolling my eyes inside my heart.

Christians often throw Christianize at people and it can be overwhelming.

The same Christians who lob *"Date Jesus"* frequently spout *"Your best days are*

ahead" and *"God has something better for your life."*

While these statements may be hopeful, they're not guaranteed. Christians can't

promise these assurances. Life may not lead to remarriage; it might bring cancer,

job loss, or a tragic car wreck. Living in a broken world means we can't predict if

our situations will improve. Misusing the verse "God works all things for good" is

unhelpful and rarely taught correctly. Imagine using it with someone who just lost a child to cancer or received devastating news about a spouse's health. Why use

it during and after a divorce?

For those of us who are divorced and seeking hope and a silver lining, it's crucial

to be discerning as we navigate dating and divorce advice. Well-intentioned friends

may offer shallow promises that aren't always accurate or helpful. The church is

flawed and people are broken. This life is hard.

So, what's next?

Here's what I discovered for myself—surround yourself with mature friends who

genuinely care for you. Seek out churches and support systems that address real

issues and the rawness of life. Personally, I've found solace in attending Celebrate

Recovery, which is similar to AA but not limited to alcoholics. Picture small groups

for church gatherings with discussions deeper and more genuine than the latest

Christian book your church assigned for your small group. It's a community of people who acknowledge their brokenness and discuss it with openness, sometimes embarrassing openness. And it is refreshing.

I once had a friend, more than a decade ago, who courageously stood up in church to share his struggles with overeating. It struck me as remarkable that someone would openly discuss such a personal challenge, and looking back, I'm grateful he did. He spoke about attending an Overeaters Anonymous class and expressed a longing for the church to be a place where such discussions could flourish. Now, after being divorced for five years, I find myself resonating with his sentiments. The church, it seems, lacks the necessary support systems. While there is ample teaching, talking, and the formation of circles, these often involve individuals who haven't experienced significant challenges themselves or at least admit it publicly. We often smile and pretend everything is ok, like admitting our challenges or personal situations would somehow make us look like failing Christians.

In many spaces, I've come to recognize a significant gap between the church and the believers it serves. It's a gap that prevents the church from effectively ministering to those in crisis. Some churches seem more focused on their systems and the people within those systems than on addressing real, broken-world issues that the flock face. There's an emphasis on telling people what books to read to make their small groups function, but what about those of us grappling with genuine crises, real-life problems that demand tangible solutions?

It's not my intention to criticize the church, although I understand that this entire chapter might be interpreted that way. Instead, I aim to speak truthfully about the reasons why divorcees often feel unwelcome and underserved in the church.

Now, let's consider singles groups within the church— the effort to minister to "newly single" members. While these ministries have good intentions, many fall short for a variety of reasons. For instance, a significant number of church single groups are designed for individuals aged 19 to 26, typically those fresh out of high school or college. However, the challenges faced by recent graduates are markedly different from those encountered by divorced or widowed adults.

Singlehood is not a universal experience; we are not all on the same journey. Many of us are emerging from or still navigating through a life crisis. Consequently, activities like pizza nights and bowling may not meet our unique needs, especially when some of us are still in the process of healing and not yet ready to embark on the dating or social scene.

In essence, there's a vital need for the church to go beyond merely playing the role of a church and instead engage in authentic ministry. I personally craved spending time with people who "got me" and knew what I was journeying through.

Secondly, we know who often gets stuck leading these single groups: 28-year-old Brad, along with his wife and their two-year-old baby. Brad might not be well-versed in ministering to divorced individuals and sometimes we pay the price for that. This divorce ministry might be his second, third, or fourth priority as an associate pastor, and he's mostly handling logistics and just trying to check the box on his "to do" list. We often have to offer grace to this situation or we can just avoid these programs altogether.

Also, some church single programs can feel like meat markets for women seeking Christian men and vice versa. There's plenty of drama and awkwardness. I won't dwell on this, but I've gathered some amusing and even creepy stories over the years. However, most divorced people I know attended once and never returned. Single ministries often provide a superficial solution to a complex problem. What is a singles ministry? Are events the solution? Are programs the answer? Those of us healing need more therapy and recovery than they need a retreat, laser tag, or a place to watch the Super Bowl.

Crisis ministry doesn't adhere to calendars and cookie cutter ministries.

If you do not feel heard with the ministries and activities in your local church, consider joining a divorce class or support group, possibly with another local church or program. Its OK, I give you permission. Some of you may be in positions where "cheating on your home church is frowned on." Its OK. God will not strike

you down or turn you into salt. It's not a sin. That much I do know.

You might relate to my experience of turning down numerous invitations to

participate in my church's busy activities. For instance, I often share a humorous

anecdote about men's ministry. It feels ironic that there's a leader overseeing the

men's ministry who feels compelled to organize events, such as a weekend retreat.

He asks men to contribute their time and effort to help run the event. Yet, the

message from the speaker at the event emphasizes the importance of spending

more time with family and being better parents. I find myself thinking, "I was already

doing a pretty good job. Why did you ask me to come here then? How much time

did we all spend putting this event all together?" Perhaps like me, you too may

decide to decline participation in such activities, choosing not to "play church." We

don't have to be drawn back into the routine of church responsibilities, but we

certainly can invest in the lives of those who are hurting, either informally or through

church-sanctioned programs.

And finally, let's not overlook the specifics for those of us further down the road to recovery. It's a bit like the journey of childbirth; we move forward, the pain fades, and we focus on raising our kids. However, let's empathize with those still on this path. Let's recall the loneliness, the pain, the soul-crushing weight, shattered dreams, and those awkward moments when someone walks into a church, bloodied and with torn clothes, limping from the wreckage of their divorce. Instead of brushing it aside or emphasizing God's value for marriages, let's acknowledge their pain. Let's be present, sitting beside them, tending to their wounds, assisting in their recovery, and assuring them that they are loved, valued, and seen. Maybe there is someone in your church journeying on your same path?

In this tough, broken world, we face hardships. It's crucial not to abandon our churches, not to forsake fellowship. When you're ready, whether crawling, walking, or running, come back to your churches. Start from the back row, slip in and out as needed until you feel prepared. Wade gradually from the shallow to the deep.

Rejoice with those being baptized, partake in communion, and genuinely love the person next to you. Be an active part of the community.

Now, I must offer an apology for critiquing the church today, but I won't apologize for advocating for the disenfranchised. I want to assure you that the frustration you endure is shared by many. Many of us have been deeply wounded by the church.

You are not alone.

Helpful Exercises

Reflecting on Church Experiences:

Compose a reflective letter addressed to the church. Share your feelings of hurt, disappointment, or betrayal. Delve into specific incidents and articulate their impact on your faith. Reflect on the type of support that would have been beneficial during this challenging time. Don't mail it. But if it ages well, use your notes for a frank and beneficial discussion with church leadership.

Identifying Supportive Church Community:

Compile a list of positive experiences within a church community or pinpoint supportive individuals. Reflect on the characteristics that contribute to a positive, nurturing environment.

List what you love about your church.

List moments members have blessed you or your family.

List the names and special traits of people you admire or look up to at church.

Forgiveness Journal:

Chronicle specific individuals that you may need to forgive and give grace to for hurtful or harmful actions. Decide today how you will pray for them and pray for your situation.

List the person's name. The core issue. How you will decide to pray for that situation and for how long.

Setting Boundaries:

Identify situations where boundaries may need to be drawn. Make a list of church activities (Frankly this is a great exercise for any area of your life) that take significant time in your life. Score them on a scale of 1-10 on:

For Church Events, Responsibilities, and Opportunities.

(Score 1-10)

Passion:

Impact:

Time:

For Personal Events, Responsibilities, and Opportunities.

(Score 1-10)

Passion:

Impact:

Time:

Income:

If answers are not 8,9,10 and/or Time is not a 2 or below… you may want to consider quitting or outsourcing.

i.e.

Mowing the Yard

Passion 3, Income 0, Impact 7, Time 2 (Maybe Outsource)

Editing Neighborhood Newsletter

Passion 7, Income 2, Impact 5, Time 2 (Maybe Pause)

Working in Youth Group

Passion 5, Impact 8, Time 4 (Maybe Pause)

Exploring Alternative Recovery Practices:

Research and delve into alternative recovery programs, such as prayer groups, meditation, Celebrate Recovery or divorce recovery programs, on or offline. These do not even need to be official programs. From neighborhood workouts to Youtube classes to peaceful hobbies. (I literally bought a boat and spending time on it might have been one of the best recovery practices I had post divorce.

Chapter Five

Grace and Divorce

"Your ex is an idiot, your friends and family abandoned you. Your world

was turned upside down after your divorce. Grace has the power to

transform even the most challenging aspects of becoming single again.

Explore the profound connection between grace and divorce. Discover the

transformative power of grace on your UnYoked journey."

What's the connection between grace and divorce? Well, it's significant. Before we delve into that connection, let's go back and ensure we're all on the same page. We need to grasp the essence of grace—its layers, meanings, and implications. Bear with me; I won't preach or claim to have mastered it, but understanding vertical and horizontal grace can truly benefit those of us who are in some messy situations and relationships.

Grace is akin to the word love, not in meaning, but in how we often define it based on context. Consider the word love; we use it to express affection for pizza, our pets, concerts, parents, children, or even a good nap. It's a broad term that requires definition and context, taking on different meanings based on situations. Similarly, grace is a multifaceted word. If I were to ask ten people for its definition, I'd likely receive ten different answers.

About ten years ago, Insight for Living conducted a street interview on grace and the responses were diverse. You can find the video on YouTube—it's fascinating. People assumed and asserted their definitions confidently, showcasing the varied perspectives even within the Christian community. You can hear worldly definitions, blank stares, and clunky attempts to explain a word we hear often but don't really "get." Grace is intriguing in the English dictionary, but for Christians, it holds deep theological significance. Despite this, even Christians may misconstrue or only partially understand it.

The term "grace" appears deceptively simple, yet its biblical importance requires a lifetime of exploration and application. It's paradoxical that a word associated with fluidity, "grace" is chosen to convey God's unfathomable love for sinners. This grace compels Him to offer salvation and absolution of sin without cost. A profound biblical definition is "unmerited favor," like a king stooping down to give a peasant a gift they neither deserve nor can earn. The Old Testament vividly illustrates grace in action.

Following the death of King Saul and his son Jonathan, David was made king over Israel. David inquired of the servants of Saul's family if anyone remained from his lineage. A servant mentioned Jonathan's son Mephibosheth, who had been injured and crippled at the age of five. When Mephibosheth was brought to David's house, he fell face down. As a descendant of Saul, he rightfully feared King David. In those times, kings often eliminated the family members of the former king to prevent them from growing up as potential threats. However, David reassured Mephibosheth, urging him not to be afraid.

David's kindness shone through as he promised to restore all of Saul's fields to Mephibosheth and appointed servants to work the land, ensuring a steady income for him. Additionally, David declared that Mephibosheth would dine at his table, just like one of his own sons. As a result, Mephibosheth lived in Jerusalem and consistently shared meals at the king's table. This exemplifies grace in action—receiving unmerited favor, getting something one doesn't deserve and can't earn.

Christians often use terms like love, grace, gospel, and salvation loosely. Similarly, phrases like "good works" or "good Christians" might be thrown around casually. It's essential to avoid such language, as there's no such thing as a "good Christian." The use of such terms often indicates a misunderstanding of grace.

Baptism, the gospel, grace, and love are interconnected aspects of our faith, forming a cohesive and harmonious whole.

In Ephesians 2:8-9, it is written, "For by **grace** you have been saved through faith; and this is not of your own doing. It is the **gift** of God, **not** a result of **works**, so that no one may boast." Notice the emphasis on "you **have been** saved." It's not a future event but something that has already happened. Your salvation is a gift from God, unrelated to your good deeds or efforts as a Christian. You can't earn it, and you don't deserve it. Let's break it down with a simple example. Imagine God is up in the heavens, holy and perfect, while we are way down here on earth. The idea that our actions could somehow elevate us from down here to up there doesn't make sense. God graciously stoops down to us, making us righteous. It's not about what we can do down here, whether we've led a life of stealing or murder or whether we followed in the footsteps of Mother Teresa. We are all equally distant from God's perfection. The thief and the saint are equally far away from God and His holiness.

In the time of Jesus, there were religious individuals who sought to control people's behavior to earn favor with God. However, Jesus rejected this notion. In Acts 15:10-11, the disciples addressed this issue, questioning why anyone would burden themselves with rules that even their ancestors couldn't bear. Their message was clear: salvation comes through the grace of the Lord Jesus, not through self-imposed regulations. So, the major takeaway of the gospel is that your salvation is a gift from God, received through faith, and not something you can achieve through your own efforts. It's a past event—you have been saved—emphasizing the grace that God extends to all, regardless of their past actions or religious achievements.

Now, some of you may be thinking, "Wait a minute. Aren't Christians supposed to be good people? Doesn't our behavior matter?" I mean, that's a logical thought if you're hearing about this grace thing for the first time. But read Titus 2:11 through 14 - paraphrased "the grace of God has appeared, bringing salvation for all people. It trains us to renounce ungodliness and worldly passions, and to live self-controlled, upright, and godly lives in the present age, while we wait for our blessed

hope—the appearing of the glory of our great God and Savior, Jesus Christ. He

gave Himself for us to redeem us from all lawlessness and to purify for Himself a

people of His own possession, zealous for good works."

So, in a nutshell, biblical grace is God giving eternal life to those who believe—

that's it. Not plus baptism, not plus good works, not reading the King James version

of the Bible, not keeping the Sabbath, not attending church, not staying married,

not looking like a good Christian. It's simple grace, unmerited favor. Is it too simple?

Well, this is why we call it the gospel. The gospel means good news. We could

never do it ourselves. It's comical even to think that we could. Yet, many of us are

still stuck in the cycle of religion and self-righteous behavior. It's pointless, fruitless,

and frankly, exhausting.

Living a religious life has been my reality for as long as I can remember. Growing

up in America, I was immersed in Christian culture from the very beginning. My

upbringing involved attending church three times a week and receiving education in a private school. This routine included biblical memorization, Bible quizzes, and the constant reinforcement of behavioral norms. The expectations were not just about living for God; they extended to demonstrating my behavior to those around me. It became a draining way of life.

However, a turning point came when I stumbled upon a book that transformed my perspective. You know the kind – the book that becomes a lens through which you see the world differently. It provided a paradigm shift, and I'll share its name shortly. Let me set the stage first.

My upbringing was deeply rooted in the church, with my dad following the Nazarene tradition, a Christian denomination that emphasized sanctification. Private school was my environment and behaviors and actions were ingrained as either right or wrong. Christian culture was preached as fervently, if not more so, than the gospel itself. Many of you might be familiar with these types of churches or have grown up in them.

The book I read delved into the concept of "grace killers" – individuals who seek to control you, using guilt to make you conform to "their standards." Extra biblical standards easily blended with God's standards or even biblical principles. Perhaps you find yourself in churches, families, or groups where this is happening right now. My heart genuinely breaks for you. The author, Chuck, made a profound statement that altered my life: **"Don't hand me your list."** Don't hand me your list of modesty. Don't hand me your church attendance policy. Don't hand me your list of movies I should watch. Don't hand me the list of how to navigate life. Don't tell me when I can get divorced. Don't tell me how long I need to wait to get married again. You work off your list, but don't hand me your list.

Those words became a mantra for me, a mindset that freed me from the constant pressure of adhering to a checklist dictating what to wear, which movies to watch, the length of my hair, attendance frequency at church, involvement in church activities, participation in small groups, study groups, volunteering, Bible studies, speech mannerisms, alcohol consumption, smoking, tattoos, and even entertainment choices. The exhaustive list of expectations imposed by Christian culture can be particularly overwhelming for women, from deciding on clothing like spaghetti straps, halter tops, bras, and pants to contemplating the acceptability of jewelry depending on the social rules of your denomination. If you find yourself weighed down by such expectations, know that you are not alone. Embracing the mindset of **"don't hand me your list"** can be a powerful step towards reclaiming your freedom in Christ.

This transformative book and the newfound mindset liberated me from the burden of unfair judgment. It also released me from the constant need to please others and adhere to societal expectations that dictate Christians should prioritize pleasing people and conforming to certain norms. But who says so? Certainly not Jesus. His mission was to liberate us from such constraints, just as he did for his disciples in Israel who were oppressed by grace killers, the Pharisees – a situation not dissimilar to what we face in today's American Christian culture.

If you haven't connected the dots yet, the prevailing Christian culture in America mirrors the environment in which the Pharisees held Israel captive. When Jesus arrived, he vehemently opposed these man-made rules and assumptions. He encouraged his followers to love him rather than conform blindly to a system. Discovering the distinction between a genuine relationship and mere religious practices, as well as understanding the variance between God and the institutionalized church with its accompanying culture, has brought about tremendous freedom.

I must admit, it took some time for me to navigate this newfound liberty. Questions arose, such as: What truly defines modesty, and how does it differ from my neighbor's perception of it? What constitutes actual sin, and how does it differ from the arbitrary lines drawn by my pastor or the opinions circulating among Christian authors, pastors, and church members? How does my involvement in church programs or volunteering for church events relate to my commitment to God and my responsibility to love my neighbors? What am I genuinely called to? Embarking on this journey, I faced challenges and encountered moments of failure. However, through it all, I gradually liberated myself from the immense pressure and guilt that had previously weighed me down.

The book "The Grace Awakening" by Chuck Swindoll is the book I mentioned earlier that profoundly impacted my life. It stands as one of only two books I've ever read cover to cover in one setting. I devoured "The Grace Awakening" immersing myself so deeply that I read the entire book in a bathtub. I can't recall if I constantly refilled it with hot water, but I emerged from that experience resembling a raisin. This book, however, held me captivated throughout.

"The Grace Awakening" provided me with a lasting lens through which I view life. It taught me a crucial lesson, which is the focus of this workbook: how to extend grace and avoid being a grace killer in someone else's life. For those of us who have experienced divorce, held our marriages in high regard, and harbored grievances against our exes or dealt with betrayals, secret-keeping, and family conflicts, the urge to speak truth, reveal facts, belittle, retaliate, and seek justice can be overpowering. Yet, worldly justice is the antithesis of grace.

While justice may seem warranted, God calls us to give grace and mercy instead. Even in our pursuit of justice, God encourages us to surrender it to Him and extend grace to others. One of my favorite Bible verses, Micah 6:8, is a constant reminder of this call for justice and mercy. I've even tattooed "Love mercy" on my right arm, the strong arm, and "Seek justice" on my left arm, the weaker one. These tattoos serve as a daily reminder to lean more towards mercy than the justice I may desire.

Each day, as I step out my door, I reflect on this choice. Understanding that controlling our tongue, one of the most challenging tasks, starts with transforming our hearts. As the proverb goes, "Out of the heart, the mouth speaks." Changing our internal selves will inevitably lead to a transformation in our outward expressions.

Our perspective, shaping how we view the world and our circumstances, influences our actions. It's crucial to recognize that this world is broken, and we yearn for the day of perfection, a concept mentioned in the Bible, particularly in the conclusion of First Corinthians. "Marathona…" It's a cry for the Lord to come quickly and bring about perfection and remove us from the challenges we face in this world.

Living in a broken world means we won't experience full justice here. God may provide some justice now or in the future, but it's a difficult reality to accept. For those of us who have gone through life-altering events like divorce, the desire for justice is intense. We may have hoped for reconciliation or even simple peace but instead we wallowed in tragedy, sometimes seeking meaning in it all.

A unique challenge of divorce I've pondered over and over, is the inability to work together with me ex to understand the truth, make sense of situations, and address the underlying reasons of our demise. Unlike those who salvaged their marriages through counseling, divorced individuals often lose the opportunity to uncover truth and gain understanding. We are no longer yoked and do not navigate the healing together. The mental complexities of making sense of all the layers and timelines of a relationship is often, frankly, impossible.

Many of us end up simplifying complex situations into statements like "John's just an ass" or "Julie's an alcoholic." The ability to unpack the truth and gain insights is often lost post-divorce. So we just simplify the complexities so we can store them on the shelves of our mind.

It's common to oversimplify things, attributing negative labels to ex-partners or enemies. Whether it's labeling someone a narcissist or creating derogatory names for an ex's new partner, it's a way to cope with the pain and disappointment. This simplification helps in moving forward, but it may not be a healthy or biblical perspective.

I confess that, in dealing with my own pain and disappointment, I found solace in labeling certain aspects and putting them on a "mental shelf." It helped me cope and move forward, but deep down, I recognize that this viewpoint is not healthy or aligned with a biblical lens. Over the past five years, I've been telling myself that I must not have known the person I married, and just concluded that I married the wrong person. While this mindset helped me heal, I acknowledge its oversimplification and the need for a more balanced and biblical perspective. My ex and I both live in a broken world and both have sinned against God and against each other. We just won't be able to agree with the "whys" and "timelines" behind it all.

Christianity emphasizes change—a new you, a born-again you. No matter what your horoscope might imply, you are not a slave to a birth date or to the actions of your past. Consider your ex-wife or ex-spouse, the one who may have caused pain and burned relationships to the ground. God loves them, Jesus died for them, and God is continuously working on them. They are not defined by their past actions, current actions, or even future actions.

Understanding God's grace makes it easier to extend grace to others.

Is horizontal grace missing in your life? You may have embraced God's vertical grace, but have you connected it in your relationships? Grace involves love, service, giving, forgiving, releasing, and affirming. It expands our capacity to love, so much so that we have no interest in keeping records of wrongs. Grace allows room to grow, room to be, and room to discover and develop.

Now, let's address forgiveness. There's a difference between grace and forgiveness. Forgiveness is the fruit of grace. Water the "grace root" and its fruit will produce forgiveness, tolerance, empathy, compassion, and kindness.

We often hear about vertical grace—the grace received from God. But what about horizontal grace? Are you demonstrating horizontally what you have received vertically?

Can you minister grace to people who don't inspire acts of kindness in you? Consider this: stoop down and embrace them.

Love that reaches up is adoration, love that reaches out is compassion, but love that stoops is grace.

You can extend grace without excusing the sin or becoming a doormat. Grace doesn't imply approval of bad behavior, nor does it enable sin. In fact, grace brings conviction to the heart of a sinner more quickly than a rebuke.

Think of someone right now—maybe your ex or someone particularly unlovely— and decide how you can stoop and embrace them. Be creative, be specific. Find a way to express grace through your words or actions, then do it. I dare you.

Now, let's explore some real-world examples quickly.

Extend grace to your spouse, keeping in mind the perspective of God's holiness. If God is at the highest level and we are below, the gap between you and your ex-spouse is minimal compared to God's holiness. You are not significantly closer to God than they are. Recognize that their souls were created and cherished by God. Their flaws and actions stem from various factors such as sin, the brokenness of the world, psychological issues, addictions, chemical imbalances, trauma, defense mechanisms, the environment they grew up in, selfish behavior that we all exhibit, and insecurities. The list is extensive. Despite the pain they caused you, offer them grace.

Now, brace yourself for a more challenging task: extending grace to their next relationship. Even if that person is labeled as a homewrecker, a gold digger, a bad parent, or obnoxious and condescending, the response remains the same—extend grace. When your ex decides to marry again, shower grace on their next spouse. Even after the dissolution of your own marriage, your children require stability. There will be plenty of vacations and holidays in the future. A joyful home for your ex-spouse, especially if you share children, is a positive thing. If they lack it, include it in your prayers.

Another area to consider is grace for your extended family, especially those who may have abandoned you or taken sides. Remember, God loves them too, and they might have found themselves in a difficult position, forced to choose between family and truth or even what's right. Offer them grace. Extend grace to your parents as well. They might have provided misguided advice, judged or shamed you. Perhaps they only received part of the story and lacked a complete perspective. Regardless, give them grace.

Here's an important point to consider: Grace for your kids. Your children might be feeling a bit overwhelmed, reacting to the changes in your family. Statistics show that they are responding to their world being turned upside down. Shower them with grace, prayers, and unconditional love. Don't be bothered by what others may think. Some might be casting judgment or offering unsolicited advice, but focus on loving your kids through it all. Provide them with grace and cover them in prayer.

Extend grace to your friends as well. Throughout the ups and downs of your marriage and divorce, it's likely that some friends have given you less-than-helpful advice or even offended you. You've likely been bombarded with various opinions and preferences, possibly causing a strain in your relationships. Remember, your friends are flawed, just like you and me. Some may have genuinely wanted what's best for you or your kids and spoke from that desire. Others might be a bit selfish or immature in certain areas. Offer them grace. Reach out, forgive, whether silently or in a planned conversation. Decide how to address the situation, but start by giving grace.

Then there's grace for your church. I dedicated an entire UnYoked Podcast episode to this topic, so be sure to listen to it for a deeper dive. Churches are made up of people, which means imperfections are inevitable. While there may be problems, there are also cultural and systemic issues within the church. Offer grace where you can and overlook past problems, if possible. Extend grace to those who may have hurt or offended you or added unnecessary drama to your life. Give the church episode a listen – it might provide some guidance.

Lastly, grace for your future relationships. Remember, hurt people hurt people, and this includes you and those you'll be dating. It also includes me. Recognize that everyone comes with their own set of baggage. Be mindful of this as you navigate future relationships. Offer grace to yourself and to others, understanding that healing is a process. Take the lessons from your past experiences and approach future relationships with a heart full of grace.

As I embarked on my journey of healing, I found myself cutting off many people from my life. At the slightest hint of a problem or exhaustion, I would simply run away, severing new, tender connections. I dismissed anyone with character traits that appeared challenging. In a somewhat humorous but also sobering revelation during one of my counseling sessions, my counselor pointed out that I needed to give second dates a chance. I realized I had been too quick to eliminate people after just one encounter.

One specific instance stands out. I adamantly declared to my counselor that I would never date someone who had an affair in their previous marriage. In response, my counselor, one of the coolest Christians I know, set his pen down, leaned back, and crossed his arms. He made me confront a truth: I expected others to extend grace for my spiritual immaturity and mistakes, but I hesitated to offer the same grace to them. With God's grace and guidance, I could change, but according to my rigid standards, they couldn't. The sting of that realization lingered and I had to ponder it for quite a while.

Of course, there are situations where caution in dating is necessary, for example, if you've experienced abuse in a past relationship or were married to an alcoholic. In those cases, it might be unwise to date someone who has a history of abusive behavior or it may not be healthy for you to re-yoke to someone who drinks.

But, I recognize that I am not perfect. I've matured over time and sought forgiveness for my past mistakes. I don't want to be defined by my errors and perhaps it's time for me to extend grace to others who have made mistakes in their own lives.

This concept of grace seamlessly connects to the idea of showing grace to your future spouse. In a world saturated with Disney princesses and movies portraying perfect soulmate relationships with happy endings, it's easy to forget that no one is perfect. Real relationships require effort and grace; there is no such thing as a flawless, happily-ever-after romance. It's a reality check that we often overlook.

For those of you who find yourselves navigating the challenging waters of a dissolved marriage, you may have been on the wrong side of history during your divorce or maybe you have done your best to handle the situation with integrity. Personally, I take pride in how I've managed the attempt to salvage my marriage, the navigation of a divorce, and the handling of the complexities of a broken family. However, regardless of how we spin the facts or engage in selective revisionist history to justify our thoughts and actions, none of us are without sin. We all fall short.

None of us are perfect. I bear the weight of my foolish actions, unwise words, and the realization of being a selfish husband, father, and a selfish man. If God, in His infinite grace, can forgive me, then who am I to withhold that grace and not pay it forward? The gift we've received is so immense that it cannot be contained in our hands; it must be shared, allowed to overflow.

I also want to address this matter directly. For some of you, extending grace, forgiving, and changing the lens through which you view others doesn't necessarily mean welcoming back an abuser, an addict, or a dangerous narcissist into your life or your family's life. However, as your heart softens and you find readiness, you can offer prayers for them. It's possible. If and when it's safe, some of you might be at that point, make that call, send that text – one that speaks kindness, absent of a confrontational attitude, free from sarcastic tones. Let's generously pour out grace. Let's choose to love even those who may seem unlovable.

Helpful Exercises

Recognizing Grace:

Write down two moments where grace was given to you from an individual. If appropriate and prudent, consider thanking them and explain how you have a new lens on the situation.

Acts of Grace Challenge:

Thoughtfully consider individuals who may benefit from grace, such as the ex-spouse, friends, or family. Explore practical ways to extend grace to these individuals, fostering a more harmonious and compassionate post-divorce environment. Write down each name and ponder opportunities where you can give unmerited favor to them (without any need for payback)

Forgiveness Letter:

Craft a forgiveness letter addressed to the ex-spouse, friends, or family members. Articulate emotions, acknowledge pain, and declare forgiveness. You most likely will not send this letter. This is for you, not them. This may be one of the hardest but most impactful exercises in this workbook. Put in the work.

Give Yourself Grace:

Engage in reflective journaling by exploring personal mistakes and shortcomings encountered during the divorce process. List out 5-10 actions or conversations you wish never happened pre and during your divorce. Write out what you learned and then write beside each one of the "FORGIVEN." Sometimes the situation does not allow for us to ask for forgiveness from certain individuals, but when/if appropriate, reach out and ask forgiveness… knowing, no matter the response, God has forgiven you.

Chapter Six

Helping Others: Divorce's Silver Lining

""God uses everything for good... but, everything is NOT good. What good

can come out of your pain? Finding a new partner is NOT the final goal

post divorce. Explore the transformative power of turning pain into

purpose. Join me in discovering the beauty within the silver lining and how your experience can be a guiding light for others."

What good can come out of tragedy? When the stains are deep and the scars are visible, when the dumpster fire of it all creates a haze around your life, how can anything good come of that? One thing that frequently amazes me is when you're inside your house and you look outside, the thunder is roaring, the lightning is coming down, it's pouring, and it feels like it's never going to end. And literally 2 hours later, the sun can be out and the birds are chirping, and the next thing you know there's sunshine and finally, no puddles. The storms of life seem so bad, but just a little bit of time, a little bit of God's grace can change the perspective of everything. And sometimes, it feels like maybe the storm never even happened.

We've talked a lot in this workbook about the different feelings you have after divorce. The fetal position, the crawling, the walking, and hopefully running. Things just get better with time. But for many of us, the pain lingers, and there are scars. But you know who ministers well to somebody in crisis? Somebody who's been in crisis. We need to find our silver linings.

I'm going to tell you a little story. My ex-wife, when we were married, was the children's minister at our church. Every Sunday morning, without fail, the phone would start ringing and it was inevitably one of the people who promised to work in childcare that were backing out of volunteering that morning. And we would sometimes log into Facebook and see "Oh, you were at that party last night, or you went to that concert, or oh look, you're in a whole other city, we can see." And so we would just laugh about it.

One of the other things we would ponder is there was an older group that were "the empty nesters." Quite frankly, we were young, in our twenties and thirties, and we would roll our eyes and talk about why didn't that older group help? They know what they're doing with kids; how come they're not putting in their time serving in the children's ministry? Well, then we became empty nesters, and I was like, "Oh, now I get it. We're tired. Now that I'm older, I don't want to help either." Once you pass through the hard parts of life, you often reflect and move on to the next phases of life.

But I want to ask you to please not forget the pains. For all you moms reading, recall the pains of childbirth – the pains of roads you have traveled down. Giving birth is painful, but once you hold that child and start raising them, the pain fades into the background. I'm saying this as a guy… I'm not an expert on childbirth but I hope you get my point. Remember that overwhelming feeling of being in the whirlwind of divorce, the car wreck feeling, and you muster enough energy to come into church. That feeling of being a mess and wanting help. There are people sitting to the right and left of you who need help or would benefit from the opportunity to come alongside you.

Statistics indicate that the failure rate after remarriage following a divorce is between 60% and 70%, while for first marriages, it's around 40%, averaging out at 50%. That is a high number and it's crucial for us to work on our own well-being and next steps so that, one day, we can extend that help to others, right?

Throughout my UnYoked podcast, I challenge the church's tendency to simplify complex problems with t-shirt theology and the lack of straightforward answers. One area where that commonly gets over simplified is Romans 8:28, "God causes all things to work together for good." There's a fundamental misunderstanding of this verse, often revolving around the belief that it's a promise meant to be fully experienced in this lifetime. When tragedy unfolds, there's a suggestion that it will ultimately lead to something good within the confines of our current life. However, these well-intentioned misconceptions and misapplications can have unintended and potentially destructive consequences for those who rely on them.

Tragedies are real and there are times of genuine suffering. Life does not always wrap up nicely like in a Disney movie. It's important to approach these tragedies with empathy and understanding... and sound theology and counseling.

The Bible teaches us that there are times for pain and sadness. The notion that God always has something better in store for us and will work everything out for good on this side of eternity isn't necessarily true. Life is unpredictable, and unfortunate events like a car wreck, illness, affairs, or even death can happen at any moment. It's crucial not to buy into the idea that God has someone or something better waiting for us.

Allow me to connect the dots... let's reflect on the commandment not to take the Lord's name in vain. We are literally sinning when we speak for God and make promises He did not make. People promising that God will make your life better can be misleading and potentially harmful. I've discussed this with several theologians, particularly in the context of Job's story. While some might point to Job being rewarded for his faithfulness, we need to be cautious. God didn't have to reward Job at all; he could have faced hardship without receiving a new wife, new children, or doubling his flock. God remains sovereign, regardless of the outcomes we experience.

In challenging times, we should be careful not to offer simplistic solutions or "T-shirt theology." In our crises, sometimes Christianese, the language of some believers, can be more damaging than helpful. It's essential to recognize the active involvement of God in our world and in our lives and that life's mysteries are not a mechanical turning of a wheel nor are they dictated by fate, karma, or luck. Instead, Paul, in his writings, often points to an unexplainable mystery and mindset "Be quiet. God's at work" and we often don't understand it all.

How God works in our lives is often beyond our understanding. We don't always know the purpose or the end result, but we trust that it is ultimately for our good, even if it doesn't necessarily feel like our individual good. It's disheartening when people misinterpret events, like a hurricane sparing one church while others crumble. We can't claim to speak for God in these situations. While God does reveal Himself miraculously at times, it doesn't give us the authority to make promises or claims that aren't grounded in truth. God sometimes allows the strip club to stand after an earthquake and not the church. It rains on the just and the unjust alike.

So, what is "truly good" if all things work out for good? The answer lies in God's transformative work in our lives, shaping us to be more like Jesus Christ. Our ultimate destiny is fully known by God, and even in the midst of uncertainty, we can find comfort in the assurance that God is actively involved in our lives, working towards a purpose that goes beyond our understanding.

To that end, He is at work in your life and yet we have free will. It is sometimes confusing how both can be true at once but know this… anything that makes you more like Christ is good, and anything that pulls you away from Christ is bad. Your idea of good and God's idea of good might not always align. While we may desire happiness, fulfillment, peace, a long life, and blessings, God works in us through everything that happens to transform us into the image of His Son… and that is one of His "Good" definitions.

Does this transformation include the worst things that happen to us? Yes. Does it include the things that hurt us deeply? Yes. Does it include times when we're heartbroken? Yes. Does it include times when we sin? Yes. Does it include the times when we doubt God? Yes. Does it include the times when we curse Him to His face? Yes.

Having a healthy view of God and His story gives us a healthy perspective on our response. Now, let me elaborate on this a bit further. Many of you, like me, grew up in a time where there could have been an unhealthy view of Scripture in your church(es) — a "me first" approach to biblical principles, aiming for personal wealth, success, and better leadership skills. This approach is prevalent in many pulpits. A "me-first" lens of how to read the Bible.

However, we need to reframe our understanding of Scripture. God's Word is essentially God telling us a story—His story. He is the great master author and storyteller. Unfortunately, we often turn it into a tool for personal gain, asking how it can help us or how we can extract principles to improve our lives.

In some churches, as we discussed in a previous chapter, pastors often make analogies out of analogies, like the David and Goliath story. They may say things like, "God can crush any Goliath in your life." However, that wasn't the primary purpose of the story. Our bookstores are filled with titles like "Your Best Life Now" and "Thriving in Abundance." These are perversions of the God story and of the theme of Scripture.

Even in our conservative churches, we often take pride in going verse by verse, and that's great—I love that style of preaching. However, sometimes in our meticulous study of individual verses, we can lose sight of the bigger picture of God's grand narrative. We find ourselves in the weeds without a clear understanding of where we stand in God's overarching story.

Many Christians struggle at this level of comprehension, failing to grasp the essence of what God is communicating. Yes, we are part of the story, and we have a designated place with instructions to follow. However, it's not as if we have a personal handbook, a "how-to-win-friends-and-influence-people" guide that we can carry around, extracting valuable insights to neatly package God and confine Him to our preferences. It's not about putting God in a box, asking Him to bless us when we check off the right boxes and avoiding certain behaviors to escape punishment.

Why are we talking about this? Because without a healthy lens of God and His story we can't frame our story and embark on healthy recovery.

Reflecting on this, recall the scene at Mount Sinai when Moses received the Ten Commandments amid smoke, lightning, and thunder. The awe-inspiring presence of God terrified the people below. Imagine taking a typical American Christian from today and placing them there 3000 years ago. Picture someone sitting at the base of that trembling mountain, expressing desires like, "I wish God would guide me on growing my business and blessing it. I really hope I can afford that boat, get my kid into a good school district, and see my preferred candidate voted into office for the benefit of our country." It becomes evident that God transcends such limited concerns. God is big. He is God. He is awesome. Our trivial wishes do not compare to His providential will.

The notion that we should merely borrow God to shape our lives according to our preferences is an unhealthy perspective. God is vast, and His story is expansive, encompassing more than our temporary, individual desires. We must recognize our place in His grand narrative and approach our faith with a broader understanding.

When faced with tragedy, consider the plight of the Israelites who endured generations of slavery. They faced challenges, and you might wonder, where was their redemption? Similarly, we go through our own trials, and we question where our silver lining is. It's essential to avoid clinging to the false hope of living happily ever after.

So, what's our path forward? How do we navigate life after surviving a crisis?

Let's begin by focusing on our church community… Yes, the place you were likely bruised post divorce. But after you have healed. When you are finally speaking from your scars and not your wounds, take the initiative to uplift and support your church and its flock. Even if you're not in a leadership role or don't consider yourself a natural speaker, you can still make a meaningful impact. Guide others toward valuable resources. You don't have to lead a class, but you can suggest what recovery paths may be helpful and point friends towards effective strategies. Your contribution, no matter how small, can make a difference in people's lives. That helping hand, that non-judgemental conversion, the listening and not talking moments can go a long way to let a brother or sister in Christ know they are heard and seen.

It's crucial for you to rediscover a sense of purpose and faith. Remember, **you are the church.** Don't solely rely on your church programs to spread love. You have the authority to minister to those in need and those around you, even outside your church. I'm not suggesting you leave your church, but some of you may find that your church isn't addressing these needs. Take initiative. We've discussed grace before, and incorporating grace into your life post-divorce is incredibly beneficial—not just for you, but for those around you.

Rise above retaliation. Rise above seeking justice for yourself. Rise above self-love alone. Instead, focus on improvement. I've emphasized this throughout. Invest time in developing yourself. Work on loving yourself. Recognize your value. By completing this workbook, you're demonstrating a commitment to self-improvement and wise recovery. Don't underestimate the impact of counseling. It might not be an instant transformation, but the effort you put in will bear fruit. We're all on a journey toward sanctification, and counseling aids in that process. Without a clear mind and without working through challenging issues, you might find yourself stumbling into your ministry. Approach counseling wholeheartedly.

Parents, first disciples are your children. Model well for them, shower them with love. They're going through a crisis too, just like you. It's essential to be aware that the statistics for children of divorced parents aren't promising, but you can greatly increase successful adaptation to their new realities. Learn from personal stories like mine. I was a bit of a helicopter parent for a while. Though I was present at almost all of my kids' events, I later realized that I wasn't modeling balance. When my children were almost adults, I gathered them in a room and offered a heartfelt apology. I admitted that I aimed to be actively involved in their lives, but I failed to demonstrate a healthy balance. I thought I was showing love by attending every event, but in reality, I was neglecting my health and finances.

There were different things that I was doing poorly. I share all this to emphasize that it's okay to seek forgiveness from your children. I personally asked them for forgiveness, acknowledging my mistakes and highlighting where I should have aimed higher. Some of you may need to do the same. We all stumble repeatedly, but pouring into your kids and demonstrating forgiveness, grace, and the humility to admit when you're wrong are all essential. Ask for forgiveness, move forward, and do the next right thing. It's never too late to start doing the right thing, even when you've made countless mistakes.

Additionally, consider the impact on a potential future spouse or partner. Imagine the blessings you can bring into a new relationship when you enter it with emotional health, having worked through your issues. Think about the love and respect you'll be able to offer. Personally, I've admitted that I didn't cherish well in my first marriage. Recognizing this, it's crucial for me to focus on cherishing well in future relationships. My next spouse stands to benefit greatly from this commitment, in contrast to my first spouse who didn't experience it. So, there's a silver lining —

someone will get it right this time. Yes, I failed, no doubt, but the opportunity to

learn and grow is invaluable.

I used to poke fun at couples who shared a joint Facebook account, thinking they

needed to cut the leash. Now, I realize that they may have faced challenges, and

it's not my place to judge. If that's their way of staying connected with friends and

family, then that's their agreement. I've become more open-minded and less quick

to pass judgment. Let me share a personal story involving my sister to illustrate

this point.

We were discussing how much more empathetic we've become over time. Let me

give an example - a younger me may have made fun of adults who collect comics.

I might have thought, "What a nerdy thing to do! Why would a grown adult choose

to spend their time and energy on these kind of hobbies?" or thought, "Why does

that couple fish all the time?" I used to be judgmental and shallow, and I admit I

did plenty of that. I believed cool people act in certain ways, while nerds act differently, and I made assumptions based on those beliefs. I've been shallow in countless ways. (I'm embarrassingly raising my hand here)

Now, having gone through some challenging experiences and becoming more attentive to people and their plights and recovery, My sister and I have adopted a phrase. "Let them freak'n fish." This phrase expresses a mindset we've embraced - a perspective that says, "Let them do what makes them happy." Whether it's collecting comic books, going fishing, or engaging in any activity that brings them peace and joy, we've learned not to judge. If it helps someone find solace or becomes a healthy hobby for them, who am I to roll my eyes or make internal or external judgments? It's our way of reminding ourselves not to be quick to judge a situation. We have NO idea what they are navigating or how they are healing.

This simple phrase, "let them freak'n fish," encapsulates the essence of our newfound empathy. The mindset serves as a reminder to avoid passing judgment and to appreciate the diverse ways people find happiness and contentment in their lives.

Extend grace generously, my friends. Shower it like confetti. Cease the relentless judgment about church attendance and attire choices. We lack the full picture of what others are enduring. Life is a myriad of journeys, each laden with challenges. Instead of casting stones based on observable behavior, acknowledge that, like you, people carry the weight of difficult experiences.

Reflect on the hardships of divorce. Holidays, once joyous occasions, can become a minefield of emotions. Picture that recently divorced individual you encounter, navigating a complex child custody schedule. This year, Christmas might be a tearfully rough day. Consider the intricacies of sharing children during the first and third weeks, juggling the responsibilities between parents. Loneliness permeates empty homes. So, let's be carriers of grace. Let's toss it into the air, liberally and without reservation. Cease the scrutiny, for we simply can't grasp the intricacies of others' struggles. Instead, let empathy guide us, recognizing that, just like us, people bear the scars of challenging experiences.

One significant change in my perspective now, something I never used to do, is avoiding simplifying divorce into merely labeling one spouse as 'bad' or 'good.' As you and I now know, divorce is a complex process. There are always two sides to every story, layers, complex layers. It's crucial to exhibit grace and love, to be a support for those going through it. Become a prayer warrior, nurturing the newfound ability to pray more profoundly than ever before.

For me, creating the UnYoked Podcast and writing became a silver lining amid the challenges of divorce. It posed the question, "What am I going to do with this experience?" As I engaged with others, listened to their pain stories, and witnessed the absence of wise counsel around them, I felt compelled to take the next step.

You can too. The harvest is plenty but the workers are few.

Helpful Exercises

Silver Lining Reflection:

I invite you to embark on a maturing inventory, recognizing the positive transformations and personal growth that have unfolded since your divorce. Delve into the newfound strengths, skills, and opportunities that have emerged.

What lenses have you gained?

Who do you see in an entirely different positive light?

What skills may you want to improve further?

Purpose Statement:

Beyond the quest for a new partner, I encourage you to craft a Purpose Statement that transcends the pain of divorce. Write out your thoughts then craft a sentence or two. Your value as a child of God is greater than your role as a wife or even as a mother. You are more than your beauty and role as a spouse or mother!

Guiding Light Letters:

We often don't fully understand issues until we ourselves are immersed in them. Think of people in your circles who were journeying through divorce or another heavy issue that you may not have walked beside them well. Are there ways to acknowledge, apologize, or make right?

Next Steps

Make a commitment today to how you will handle issues of friends pondering or navigating a divorce. What key phrases, resources, motos, will you want to remember to pass along? Write down monumental moments and key concepts that you will want to remember years from now.

Key Scriptures

Make a commitment today to how you will speak into friends pondering or navigating a divorce. What verses did you cling to? What scripture will you want to remember (maybe even memorize) to pass along? Write them down.

Embark on this radiant journey of self-discovery, empowerment, and purpose, knowing that each exercise brings you closer to a life filled with joy, resilience, and the radiant glow of a renewed spirit.

Epilogue

As you reach the final pages of this Christian Divorce Recovery Workbook for Women, consider this not an end but a new beginning. Your journey through these chapters has been a testament to your strength, resilience, and the transformative power of faith.

In closing, remember that healing is a continuous process. Embrace the lessons learned, cherish the newfound self-awareness, and carry the light you've discovered into the next chapter of your life. This workbook is not just a guide but a companion, offering solace and wisdom to support you on your ongoing path to recovery.

As you embark on this next phase, may you find comfort in the knowledge that you are not alone. Your story is unique, and its chapters are still being written. Cherish the growth, embrace the challenges, and let the lessons learned guide you toward a future filled with hope, purpose, and the promise of a new, empowered you.

Remember, you are resilient, worthy, and deserving of a life filled with joy and fulfillment. Your journey continues, and the best chapters are yet to come.

With faith, resilience, and a heart filled with hope,

Todd Turner

7-Days Devotional

on

Unyoked Living: Living a Life on Mission

The 7-Days Devotional on "Unyoked Living: Living a Life on Mission" serves as a compassionate and faith-based resource for those navigating life after divorce. With its daily readings, prayers, and reflections, the devotional offers guidance and support to individuals looking to heal, find hope, and live purposefully amid the challenges of divorce. By embracing the perspective of unyoked living, it encourages individuals to embark on a new chapter with a sense of mission and purpose, all while being grounded in Christian principles and spiritual growth. This approach can provide a source of strength and comfort for those seeking to navigate the complexities of life post-divorce.

Day 1

Topic: Losing Friends In A Divorce

Memorize: Proverbs 17:17 (NIV)

"A friend loves at all times, and a brother is born for a time of adversity."

Read: Proverbs 18:24 (NIV)

"One who has unreliable friends soon comes to ruin, but there is a friend who sticks closer than a brother."

Getting divorced is a big event that affects many parts of our lives, including our bonds. The hard truth about divorce is that you will lose some people along the way. Let's face it, these losses can be excruciating, and they may have a significant effect on your friends and family. There is a bright side to all of these deaths. The wise words in Proverbs 18:24 say that a true friend always loves, and Proverbs 17:17 says that a true friend stays closer than a brother. Through this challenging time, keep an eye on who is by your side. When things go wrong, true friends show who they are.

Going through a divorce changes a lot of things, and friendships can end for a number of reasons. Friends may drift apart because of moving, money problems, changes in routines, or even the difficulty of choosing sides in a split. For some people, the pain is worse when their mate is also their best friend.

Friendships after a divorce can be tricky because people are dealing with fear and sadness. Some people may pull away because they don't know how to help and are afraid they will say or do the wrong thing. Having to choose sides can put pressure on friendships, and after a divorce, people may form or drift apart in ways that were not expected.

When a couple gets divorced, it can be challenging for their friends to stay friends. When your marriage ends, your close friends don't know how to handle the new circumstances. They may not always be able to see past their relationships, which can put them in awkward situations where they have to pick sides or keep their friendships separate.

After these losses, it's essential to plan how to build a new group that will help each other. Know that it's okay if the people you hang out with change. Find friends who are closer than a brother and enjoy the realness of genuine relationships. Be willing to try new things and make new friends that fit with your journey after the split.

Key Point:

Remember that getting over a divorce means learning to understand, accept, and find a new balance in your social groups. Trust that God is with you every step of the way. He is the best friend and sticks closer than a brother.

Prayer:

Heavenly Father, help me find comfort in Your presence as I deal with the difficulties of losing friends after a split. Please give me the knowledge to know which friends are accurate, the strength to deal with loss, and the courage to make new friends. I pray in the name of Jesus. Amen.

Day 2

Topic: Facing Loneliness with The Shepherd

Memorize: Psalm 34:18 (NIV)

"The Lord is close to the brokenhearted and saves those who are crushed in spirit."

Read: Psalm 23 (NIV)

Loneliness can be a pervasive companion, especially during the challenging journey of divorce recovery. In these moments, it's crucial to turn to the Shepherd, who promises to be close to the brokenhearted. Psalm 23 beautifully paints a picture of the Lord as our Shepherd, guiding, comforting, and providing. Let's explore how this passage speaks to us when loneliness strikes. The opening words declare, "The Lord is my shepherd; I shall not want." Recognize that, in your loneliness, God takes on the role of a caring shepherd. He knows your needs and is committed to providing them. Loneliness often leaves us feeling broken and weary. However, the Shepherd promises to restore our souls. Through prayer, reflection, and seeking God's presence, find restoration for your weary soul.

Loneliness can lead to confusion and despair. Yet, the Shepherd guides us in righteous paths. Turn to His Word for direction and clarity as you navigate the challenges of divorce recovery. Even in the darkest valleys of loneliness, take comfort in the Shepherd's presence. He promises to be with us, offering solace and strength. Spend time in prayer, knowing that God is close to you. Despite loneliness, the Shepherd prepares a table for us. This signifies His provision and abundance. Seek the nourishment of His Word and the fellowship of supportive friends and family.

Loneliness may make you feel empty, but the Shepherd promises an overflowing cup of blessings. Recognize the blessings around you, cultivating gratitude and a positive perspective. Ultimately, the Shepherd invites us to dwell in His house forever. As you face loneliness in divorce recovery, remember that your ultimate home is in God's presence. Find solace and security in the assurance of eternal companionship.

Key Point:

In the face of loneliness, remember that you are not alone. God, your Shepherd, walks with you on this journey of divorce recovery, guiding you, comforting you, and leading you to a place of healing and hope.

Prayer:

Heavenly Father, in moments of loneliness, I turn to You, my Shepherd. Thank You for the promise of Your presence, guidance, and restoration. Help me find comfort in Your Word and the support of those around me. In Jesus' name, I pray. Amen.

Day 3

Topic: Embracing Change

Memorize: Isaiah 43:18-19 (NIV)

"Forget the former things; do not dwell on the past. See, I am doing a new thing! Now it springs up; do you not perceive it?"

Read: Isaiah 43:16-21 (NIV)

It can be hard to let go of the past, the memories, and the pain while getting over a divorce. For this reason, Isaiah 43:18–19 tells us to welcome change, let go of the old, and see the new things God is doing in our lives. The first few lines of

Isaiah 43 talk about how God is always there to help His people through life's problems. The reference to the Red Sea splitting is a miracle that shows how powerful and saving God is. It's a warning that the same God who moved things in the past is still at work today. Problems may have happened in the past for you, but just like God made a way for the Israelites to cross the sea, He is making a way for you now. "Forget the former things; do not dwell on the past." What these words say encourages us to let go of the past, forgive, and let God heal the hurts that divorce has left behind. It can be hard to let go of the past, but God wants us to so that we can fully enjoy the new season He has planned.

"Look, I'm up to something new!" It's coming up now; can't you see it?" God is asking us to see the new work He is doing in us. It takes a change of viewpoint, a willingness to look past the hurt and pain, and the knowledge that God is working to make something beautiful out of the ashes of our brokenness.

"I am making a way in the wilderness and streams in the wasteland." The forest stands for the complex and lonely times we go through while getting over a divorce. But God says he will make a way and bring streams of water in the middle of the dryness. He not only leads us through the rough territory, but He also gives us life through His living water.

As we let go of the past and accept change, we make room for God's new work in our lives. This sets us up to live a life on purpose. Being on this journey isn't just about getting better; it's also about becoming channels for God's love, grace, and redemption. As we work through the healing process after a divorce, we can praise God and show how He can change our lives. The most important thing is to remember that getting over a divorce is not the end but the start of a new path. God is clearing a path and giving comfort in the middle of a desert. As we let go of the past and see His latest work, He calls us to live a missionary life, one that shows how faithful He is, how He heals, and how beauty can come from pain.

Key Point:

It's important to remember that getting over a divorce is not the end but the start of a new path. God is clearing a path and giving comfort in the middle of a desert. As we let go of the past and see His latest work, He calls us to live a missionary life, one that shows how faithful He is, how He heals, and how beauty can come from pain.

Prayer:

Lord, help me let go of the past and trust in the new things You are doing in my life. Guide me as I embark on this journey of unyoked living.

Day 4

Topic: Finding Your Identity in Christ

Memorize: 2 Corinthians 5:17 (NIV)

"Therefore, if anyone is in Christ, the new creation has come: The old has gone, the new is here!"

Read: Philippians 3:7-14 (NIV)

People who have been through a breakup often feel like the pain of the past defines them. Brokenness can make us lose sight of our sense of self-worth and meaning.

But in the middle of this arduous journey, God invites us to rethink who we are in Christ—a new identity that gives us the strength to live a life on a mission.

The words in 2 Corinthians 5:17 give hope to people who are hurt. "Therefore, if anyone is in Christ, the new creation has come: The old has gone, the new is here!" These words say something significant: in Christ, our past doesn't hold us back. The scars of divorce don't define who we are. Instead, we are called "new creations" because of what Christ did to save us. His kindness, forgiveness, and never-ending love have become a part of who we are.

As you go through the complex process of getting over a divorce, it's important to remember that your identity is not based on your relationship status or the events that led to the divorce. You are not marked by the end of your marriage or the mistakes you made in the past. You are marked by the unchanging love of God and the power of Christ's sacrifice to change things.

Getting ideas from Philippians 3:7–14, we see that the apostle Paul put knowing Christ ahead of his past accomplishments. The goal of his life becomes clear: to become like Christ. In the same way, your job is to accept and live out your new character in Christ. To do this, you have to choose to stop dwelling on the past and start enjoying the present, from judging yourself to accepting God's forgiveness.

To live on a mission after a divorce, you need to know how much God loves you and let that love flow into every part of your life. It means forgiving yourself and others, knowing that Christ's sacrifice for our sins covers all of them. Your job is to walk with confidence in your new identity, showing how God's kindness can change things.

Key Point:

As you get over your breakup, think about how your story will affect others. Your struggles, successes, and experiences can be a sign of God's faithfulness and healing. By living with a purpose, you not only give your pain meaning but also become an inspiration to people who are going through similar things.

Prayer:

Heavenly Father, I thank You for how Your love can change things. To fully understand who I am now in Christ, please help me. As I get over my divorce, my life on a mission for you gives me strength and a sense of purpose. Tell other people my story to provide them with hope and healing. Amen

Day 5

Topic: Unyoking from Bitterness

Memorize: Ephesians 4:31-32 (NIV)

"Get rid of all bitterness, rage, and anger, brawling and slander, along with every form of malice. Be kind and compassionate to one another, forgiving each other, just as in Christ God forgave you."

Read: Colossians 3:12-14 (NIV)

"Therefore, as God's chosen people, holy and dearly loved, clothe yourselves with compassion, kindness, humility, gentleness, and patience. Bear with each other and forgive one another if any of you has a grievance against someone.

Forgive as the Lord forgave you. And over all these virtues put on love, which binds them all together in perfect unity."

Bitterness can easily take hold of a hurt heart and make it hard to carry out the goal God has for us. Letting go of it is a vital part of living a life on a mission. Paul, the Apostle, writes a powerful message to the Ephesians about how important it is to let go of anger. He tells us in Ephesians 4:31–32 (NIV) to "Get rid of all malice, wrath, and anger, as well as all fighting and slander." Let's be kind and sensitive to each other and forgive each other, just as God forgives you in Christ.

This Bible verse shows how forgiveness can change things. Along with forgiving others, it tells us to stop being angry and start being kind and caring, just like Christ did for us. One of the most important things we have to do as Christians is show kindness, love, and forgiveness to people who have hurt us.

Colossians 3:12–14 (NIV) gives us more information on how to break free from anger. As God's chosen people, we are to dress ourselves in traits that bring people together and help them heal. This part of the text says, "*Therefore, as God's holy and beloved people, put on compassion, kindness, humility, gentleness, and patience.*" Be patient with each other and forgive each other if someone has hurt you. Do what the Lord did and ignore them. Put love on top of all these principles because love is what holds them all together perfectly.

Bitterness often starts when people don't want to let go of their hurts and complaints. But these texts make it clear that the call to forgive doesn't depend on what the other person did. Instead, it comes from the fact that we are God's chosen and deeply loved children. Knowing how much God forgives us gives us the grace to forgive others, too. We can no longer be held back by anger because of this act of grace. It frees us to carry out our goals of love, healing, and reconciliation.

Key Point:

In divorce recovery, unyoke yourself from bitterness. Extend forgiveness as Christ forgave you. Bitterness hinders your mission. Today, choose kindness and compassion.

Prayer:

Lord, help me release bitterness and choose forgiveness. Fill my heart with kindness and compassion, allowing me to live out the mission You have for me.

Day 6

Topic: Building a Foundation on Christ

Memorize: Matthew 7:24 (NIV)

"Therefore everyone who hears these words of mine and puts them into practice is like a wise man who built his house on the rock."

Read: Matthew 7:24-27 (NIV)

Welcome to another day of exciting discussion. It is essential to build a strong base on Christ as you strive to recover through the divorce process. Jesus used the example of building a house on a rock in Matthew 7:24–27 to teach us a profound lesson about how important it is to have a strong base. Think about two builders: one who works on rocks and one who works on sand. A wise person who not only hears what Christ says but also does what he says is like someone who builds on rock. The house stays strong even when storms and winds blow because the base is strong.

When it comes to getting over a divorce, "building on the rock" means firmly rooted in the teachings and principles of Christ. It means not only hearing His words but also putting them into practice in our daily lives. When we go through hard times in life, like getting divorced, this foundation gives us power, stability, and the ability to bounce back.

Putting your faith in Christ is more than just an intellectual or theoretical exercise. That's the main thing. It needs deliberate effort. In order to get over a divorce, we need to actively seek advice from God's Word and live our lives in line with His rules. To do this, we need to forgive, love, care, and promise to carry out the task He has given us. We make sure that our reaction to the difficulties of divorce is based on what Christ taught by "building on the rock." This base gives us the strength to handle the spiritual, emotional, and practical parts of recovery with faith, wisdom, and strength. The base can stand up to the storms and give you a stable place to live your life on purpose, even when things are hard.

Along your path to healing from your divorce, let Christ be the rock on which you build your life. Pay attention to what He says, think about it, and then do what He says. By doing this, you'll find the strength and purpose you need to live a life on a mission based on Christ's unbreakable foundation.

Key Point:

Establish your foundation in Christ during divorce recovery. As you live a life on mission, build upon the solid rock of His teachings. Today, commit to putting His words into practice.

Prayer:

Lord, be the foundation of my life. Help me build upon Your teachings and withstand the challenges of divorce recovery as I live out the mission You have for me.

Day 7

Topic: Walking in Hope

Memorize: Romans 15:13 (NIV)

"May the God of hope fill you with all joy and peace as you trust in him, so that you may overflow with hope by the power of the Holy Spirit."

Read: Psalm 42:5-11 (NIV)

"Why, my soul, are you downcast? Why so disturbed within me? Put your hope in God, for I will yet praise him, my Savior and my God."

The mental toll of divorce can be too much, and the path may look hard. The basis of our hope, on the other hand, is not tied to the things that are constantly changing but to the fact that God is the same. Romans 15:13 is a bright light of hope in the storm of getting over a breakup. It points us to the God of hope and makes us aware of how much He wants to fill our hearts with joy and peace. This divine infusion doesn't depend on how predictable our circumstances are; it's a sign of how trusting God in the middle of life's uncertainties can change things.

When the poet cries out in Psalm 42, their words echo with this hope. Here, we see an open and honest picture of inner turmoil: the soul struggling with feelings of sadness and unease. Even though the psalmist is having a hard time emotionally, they refuse to give up and give in to hopelessness. Instead, he tells everyone who is going through a rough time emotionally to put their hope in God.

When the psalmist writes about hope, it's not just passive optimism or wishful thought. It goes beyond just hoping for something to happen and turns into a sure belief based on God's unwavering promises and trustworthiness. It is a choice to think that God stays the same; his character doesn't change, even when bad things happen.

When getting over a breakup, when feelings are strong, and the unknown is significant, the call to put our hope in God becomes a lifeline. It's an invitation to look away from the rough waves of our lives and toward the stable base that is the One who made the world. This hope isn't an escape from reality; it's a sure belief that God will keep His word, His promises will stand, and His power to redeem will make beauty out of ashes.

As we work through the healing process of a divorce, may we find comfort and strength in the fact that our God does not change? Let us trust that He is the God of hope and that He will fill us with joy and peace as we trust Him.

Key Point:

As you conclude this devotional, walk in hope. Trust in the God of hope, who fills you with joy and peace. Allow His hope to overflow in your life as you continue your mission.

Prayer:

Lord, fill me with joy and peace as I trust in You. Let Your hope overflow in my life, guiding me on the mission You have prepared for me. Amen.

Author's Note

A giant thank you to my sister, Tanya, and to Harmony for helping me smooth the rough edges, for offering sound advice, and for being graceful along the way.

About the Author

Todd Turner is a Faith-Based Non-Profit Consultant by day and primarily sleeps in North Texas where he just ended his full time stint of raising three kids and kicking them all out of the nest…. gently… with a stick…. but gently. He loves water and his dream evening is enjoying his music, cigars, and friends looking out over a lake or an ocean.

Todd grew up reading Lewis Grizzard and owns all his books… between reading, consuming podcasts, and morning yoga… he fills the rest of his day helping his children and his clients grow and continue to be life-long learners.

More Resources

Listen and Subscribe to the UnYoked Living Podcast on Youtube or your favorite podcast provider.

Printed in Dunstable, United Kingdom